Praise for *Yoga for the Brain!*

"I love *Yoga for the Brain!* It is a great way to relax, unwind and play. **Even better, research shows that games like these can have a mind-body benefit no matter how old you are. Sign me up for more!**"
—*Camille Leon, Founder, Holistic Chamber of Commerce*

"Never before have I seen such a book, with word search puzzles, secret messages, and even more for the reader to enjoy! More than just a word search puzzle book, it's also packed with facts and information. Sitting down with the book is a great way to relax and stretch those brain muscles. I can see why the puzzles are considered 'yoga for the brain!' **This book is highly recommended for those looking for puzzles, relaxation, inspiration, and enjoyment!**"
—*Carla Trueheart for* Readers' Favorite

"*Yoga for the Brain* is inspirational, relevant, and fun! The puzzles are challenging in a good way, and the messages are insightful and meaningful. It's well worth your time. **I highly recommend it to everyone looking for something uniquely uplifting.** It provides an all-around positive experience anyone can benefit from. The books encompass food for thought and food for the soul!"
—*Brenda Krueger Huffman, Publisher,* Women's Voices Magazine

"Cristina Smith's **fun and easily accessible works brilliantly blend quantum consciousness-based science with profound philosophical wisdom.**"
—*Dr. Amit Goswami, Quantum Physicist and bestselling author of* The Self-Aware Universe

"While I've never actually heard the term "yoga for the brain" before, it makes total sense. This book easily fulfills the mental and spiritual aspects of a Yoga practice. **So much more than a puzzle book, the fun facts, history, and education lining the pages make Yoga for the Brain books a unique treasure.** I highly recommend it for an entertaining and enlightening experience!"
—*Sheri Hoyte for* Reader Views

"Cristina Smith thinks deeply and writes with the kind of simplicity and clarity that only comes from an almost cellular attunement to her subjects. Without pretense or posturing, she uplifts me."
—*Steven Forrest, author of* The Inner Sky

"Everything Cristina writes about in her books is about our choice of what to do with the great gift of life we have been given. She has experienced in her own life the power of the spirit to transform and allow her to tap into her energy and enthusiasm to help others become all they can be. Puzzles are half of what these books are about. The other half is the commentary Cristina provides that helps us to learn to live fully in this present moment. Highly recommended!"
—*Dr. Russell Fanelli, Professor Emeritus, Western New England University*

"Highly Recommended!"
—*The Wishing Shelf, UK*

The *Yoga for the Brain*™ series has earned more than a dozen literary awards in the United States and United Kingdom. Have fun discovering why by looking inside!

Life Wisdom Word Search
Yoga for the Brain™

Cristina Smith
Rick Smith

A POST HILL PRESS BOOK
ISBN: 978-1-64293-475-5

Life Wisdom Word Search:
Yoga for the Brain™

Post Hill Press
New York • Nashville
posthillpress.com

Published in the United States of America

Table of Contents

Prepare to Get Happy

What do jazz, the meaning of life, poetry, and puzzles all have in common?

A poet peers out her window across a city street. There's a dreamy, faraway look in her eyes. Suddenly a jolt runs through her body. She rushes back to her desk and jots down the next line of her poem.

Where did that line come from?

The jazz trumpeter gazes into space as the pianist finishes his solo. Suddenly, a cascade of notes pours from his horn. The passage is elegant. He's never played it that way before. He is as surprised and delighted as his audience.

Where did he get that melody?

Even if we are not artists, all humans are capable of extraordinary creativity. Maybe we are faced with some dilemma in life. In a flash, the famous "lightbulb" lights over our heads. We have found an answer that works. But how did we come up with it? Did we find that answer in the same way that we balance our checkbook or calculate our taxes? Not at all—it is an entirely distinct process, and much more mysterious. The difference is that we have conscious knowledge of checkbook calculations, while with any kind of true creativity, we really have no idea where those answers come from. Poof—they simply appear. They are not there, then they are. We did it, somehow—but we don't know quite how.

There is more: when that little everyday miracle happens, we feel happy. We feel charged with life. Another way to express it is that we are simply having fun. If we think about that line for a moment, it can carry us straight down into the heart of an ancient mystery. We all have a larger self. That larger self is the deep well from which these kinds of flashes arise. And when that happens, it also energizes us. Joy bubbles up. Whether we label that deep well the psyche, the soul, or the unconscious mind, we know that it is there. The existence of human creativity simply proves it.

With our poet and our jazz trumpeter, we asked the question: where did their inspiration come from? That same deep well is our answer. It is that sea of luminous lightbulbs upon which our conscious minds float like a bobbing cork.

And whenever we part the veil between us and that vast inner realm, energy pours into us. We light up. We smile. We are glad to be alive. Even when we do it in simple, playful ways, we have plugged into the ancient battery of life itself.

I invite you to sit down with this edition of *Yoga for the Brain,* let your creative imagination guide you, and be prepared to get really happy.

—Steven Forrest, author of *The Inner Sky*

Cristina Smith & Rick Smith

The Meaning of Life

What is wisdom? How do we gain it? Is what everyone considers wisdom the same? Does it only come with age? Does the famous phrase *out of the mouths of babes* actually mean anything? Once we throw the word *life* into it, we're really looking at the big questions. In a puzzle book? Really?

As humans, we are all on the same quest to some degree or another. We all want to discover the elusively magical meaning of life. Myths and legends have been built around this question. It is the subject of deeply meditative contemplation and prayer. Philosophers and priests of every belief and faith debate the answer. It's the holy grail of self-knowledge.

Many want to tell us the answer and have us join their parade regarding life's meaning. Others would simply say the answer is love, or oneness, or "42." Ultimately, though, deep down in our inner sanctums, we already know the answer. The meaning of life is to live a meaningful life. Our exceptionally personal, exquisitely individual, different from everyone else's, life. One filled with purpose, whatever that looks like for each of us.

Searching for our purpose takes us on the journey of our own life story in which we are the main character, the hero. How we star in that role is up to us. We seek meaning, venture out, face trials and conflicts, eventually triumph over adversity, and are then richly rewarded with priceless treasure, both in our inner and worldly lives. Then we're on to the next quest.

Some find purpose in family, others careers, and others profoundly mystical spiritual development. Many must focus on the basics of survival day-to-day. Some of us are digital nomads and others have lived most of their lives in their family home, like generations before them. Purpose changes with individuals and sometimes time.

In our own unique way, the meaning of life is *yes*. What we say *yes* to in our lives is what our lives become.

Yes can open lots of new doors and opportunities. It can also shoot us in the foot even before we begin. There are those habitual *yeses* that perhaps perpetuate a cycle of familiar pain. Some of us continue to say yes to our relationships, businesses, and circumstances long after our hearts and souls really want to say no. Letting go by saying no is hard. What do you say yes to in life?

With such affirming consequences, it is important that we think about, choose, and discern our yeses. What follows the word *yes* matters immensely. *Yes...but* really means "I wish I could say no." In these circumstances, a firm "no" works best in creating the world we want for ourselves. Sometimes saying no is really saying yes to ourselves. In our quest for our meaning of life, we have said yes to many opportunities and have also had the stalwart courage and fortitude to say no.

When yes is followed by *please* or *and*, we keep moving on and expand on the concept of yes. *Yes and* or *yes please* send a clear message to the world. We have made a choice and embraced something. It is not just some default, path of least resistance, deciding-by-not-deciding moment.

We are delighted you have said "**yes**" to following the fun treasure map of wisdom, solving the puzzles, and decoding the secret messages within. You've said "**yes**" to exercising both sides of your brain, reducing stress, and enjoying moments of relaxing mindfulness. You've said "**yes**" to boosting your health and happiness through the power of positive play. And you've said "**yes**" to sipping from the cup of your inner holy grail through these wisdom stories and considering your own *once upon a time*, leading to what can become an ever unfolding *happily ever now*.

Be the star of your own life.

Wisdom comes in many forms and flavors. Our contributors' perspectives span most of a century: the elder was born in the 1920s, the youngest in 2012. Read each puzzle to discover a broad spectrum of viewpoints. Explore the meaning of life through the various stages and ages. From New Zealand, to Arkansas, to Germany, to India, to the UK, to Uganda; from poets to jazz musicians to teens, to chaplains to sailors to healers—enjoy taking a peek into other ordinary yet inspiring heroic lives and journeys. What chapter of your experience would you contribute? Your own hero's journey is calling. Your quest continues. Share your wisdom.

Happy puzzling!

Let's Play!

Have Fun!

How to Play

A word search puzzle consists of letters placed in a grid. Some of the letters form words, others don't. The object of this game is to find and mark all the words hidden inside the grid that appear in the accompanying word list.

The words may be placed horizontally, vertically, or diagonally, and arranged forward or backward. They may share letters with other words.

Hidden within the puzzle is a secret message created by the letters that are not used in any word within the grid. The key to decoding it is underneath the text of the reading.

The blank lines are where you will place the letters discovered once the word search phase of the puzzle is complete. Starting from the top left corner of the puzzle grid and proceeding left to right, line-by-line, place each unused letter on the blank line in the order it appears. When solved, the Life Wisdom message associated with the reading magically appears!

❀ *Cristina Smith & Rick Smith*

How to Find the Words

*Knowing where to start is sometimes
the key to the solution.*

There is no one right way to solve word search puzzles. It's individual. Your unique brilliance will reveal your perfect way forward. Word search puzzles are a wonderful way to play with your brain and help increase its flexibility. Experiment with these different strategies and notice how it feels when doing each. It is likely that one approach will feel more natural.

What's great about playing with your brain in this context is that it is a no-risk proposition. Nothing critical is on the line. There is no deadline. No one else will be judging your performance. It is the perfect laboratory in which to do research on yourself. A whole brain approach could look something like this:

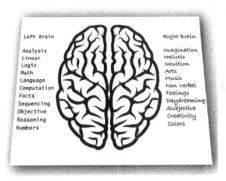

Start with the right-brain intuitive approach. Read the story. Scan the grid and see what words you notice first. Circle them and cross them off the list. It is interesting to make a note of the ones that pop out as an indicator of your current state of being.

Take a look at the word list and then look again at the grid and see what else reveals itself. Consider picking out a word and see if you are able to find it by shifting your perspective.

Next, move to the left-brain logical strategy. A common tactic for finding all the words is to go through the puzzle left to right (or vice versa) and look for the first letter of the word. After finding the letter, look at the eight surrounding letters to see whether the next letter of the word is there. Continue this system until the entire word is found.

The step-by-step method approaches the word list in order. It's helpful to skip over the ones that are elusive at the moment and come back to those words later.

To finish, switch on the right-brain intuitive technique again. Which words did you have a hard time finding? Notice anything interesting about them? Isn't it fascinating what we see and don't see?

Get to know yourself in different states of mind.
New perspectives emerge.

Colorful Tip

Many people use a pencil to circle found words and then cross or check them off the list. That works well, especially if you have a good eraser. However, the grid looks a bit chaotic when all of the word list is found. As a colorful tip, use a highlighter felt-tip pen to identify found words in the grid. It can make it easier to recognize which letters remain unused when decoding the secret message.

Cristina Smith & Rick Smith

About the Life Wisdom Messages

Each puzzle includes a unique short story shared by one of our sixty inspiring contributing authors. They range in age from seven to ninety-four, offering us a slice of wisdom from diverse perspectives. After the puzzle section, you will briefly meet each author and be able to find out more about them at LifeWisdomWordSearch.com.

Some keys to the mysteries of inner wisdom may be unlocked while playing with the magic of word search. These puzzles are not mind-numbingly difficult. They are designed to stretch your mind and perspective, like a yoga pose.

Each puzzle creates specific benefits. First, reading initiates the overall focus of the story. The carefully selected word list supports different facets of the theme. Solving the puzzle itself improves whole brain health function and flexibility. Finally, the deciphered Life Wisdom reveals a powerful affirmation that can embed these positive messages into the essence of everyday life.

Have fun solving all of these deliciously unique puzzles and inspiring secret messages!

Start with Self-Love

Life can sometimes throw us a curveball. The unexpected happens. Things don't always feel good. People let us down or things we wished for don't come to fruition. We can be positive, optimistic, hard-working, kind, and loving. And still, life happens and sometimes it hurts.

To navigate through these times, be gentle with yourself.

Life can be a lot to handle sometimes. There are those surprise twists and turns and detours and roundabouts. Regardless of the curves, the one person you may always count on to have your back is you. You are deserving of your compassion. You are worthy of your self-care and self-love. When times get tough, the thing to remember is that you're human and you're doing the best that you can.

When those tough moments arise, as they will, take a deep breath. Remember that you will get through this. You can do so with tender, loving care. The way you show up for yourself during these challenges makes those rough times just a little bit easier. Your self-support carries you more swiftly and lovingly through to the other side.

Be the loving foundation that you can always fall back onto.

—*Shari Alyse*

Life Wisdom:

__ __   __ __ __   __ __ __   __ __ __

__ __ __ __ __ __   __ __   __ __ __

__ __ __ __ __ __ __   __ __ __ __   __ __ __ __ __ __

__ __ __

```
C U R V E S D E E P C S D T H
A H E N L O S V E A R N Y N G
L U O U O I R F R U I T I O N
Y M G I R I S E O K V E O I I
S A Y P E O T T D U R P H S V
E N R S M E E A S N T L T S O
D U F I E D S M D I E O A A L
S E R E M E I M M N W T E P T
Y H S P B O T I R S U T R M S
L T A E E U S A U R A O B O E
T N T R R T T P G E H A F C B
F N A N I V P E V I T I S O P
I N S C Y O I T H S V F L E S
W Y H T R O W N I A N A U O Y
S E L T N E G G G E E L N S E
```

Alyse	Foundation	Self
Best	Fruition	Shari
Breath	Gentle	Support
Care	Human	Surprise
Compassion	Kind	Swiftly
Curves	Loving	Tender
Deep	Navigate	Turns
Deserving	Optimistic	Twists
Detours	Positive	Worthy
Easier	Remember	You

2 Find Peace Beyond Turmoil

As humans, we are able to choose how we want to respond to life. Even in the midst of turmoil, chaos, or difficulty, we can choose peace. No matter how tough the situation, we can respond intentionally rather than react from fear. Responding takes practice and cultivation. The easiest way to assure we are responding is to take a breath and consider which choice is best before acting. We have the right and ability to be at peace no matter what.

Choosing peace in the face of unrest, uncertainty, and upheaval calms us and raises our vibration. This benefits everyone whose lives we touch. We can be one-person poster children of peace by the way we live. We can be the change we want to see in the world.

I recently had a healing journey with pancreatic cancer. Inner peace was a huge part of my healing strategy. I focused on how I wanted to feel and ways to flourish, regardless of what was happening in the moment.

God and the angels helped me every step of the way. I often was flooded by grace and a deep sense of inner peace for which I am so grateful. The good news is that you can be too, dear heart. All you need to do is ask for Divine assistance and allow it to permeate your life. Respond intentionally to life. Choose peace.

—Janette Stuart

Life Wisdom:

__ __ __ __ __   __ __   __ __ __   __ __ __ __ __

__ __ __ __ __ __ __ __ __   __   __ __ __ __ __

__ __   __ __ __ __   __ __ __   __ __ __ __   __ __

__ __ __ __   __ __ __ __   __ __

```
S E N S E S I A R E N N I D P
D N O P S E R E B A C E O I I
S T O E H H E A L I N G N E L
A S S I S T A N C E L T O O V
I H P N T O R P G C E I I O M
G T S E P A O E R N P C T A N
I R N I E D V H T A O N A Y I
C A A H R D I I C S C O R E S
J U O C M U O V T S O T B T P
O T E T E N O R I L O P I W A
U S L K A T A L H N U F V C H
R E P L T T A T F H E C O A E
N F L L E S L E G N A I F L A
E Y E G W L U F E T A R G M R
Y I Y T H M E B R E A T H S T
```

Ability	Flourish	Peace
Angels	God	Permeate
Assistance	Grace	Poster
Benefits	Grateful	Practice
Breath	Healing	Raises
Calms	Heart	Respond
Choose	Inner	Sense
Cultivation	Intentionally	Strategy
Deep	Janette	Stuart
Divine	Journey	Vibration

3 A Courageously Beautiful Life

Fear and courage. Two sides of the same coin.

Fear is a natural and essential instinct that helps us survive. Without fear we would surely make poor decisions that could jeopardize our health and safety. Yet fear can also hold us captive and keep us from taking chances that could lead to greater joy. The fear of a broken heart can make us not love as deeply. The fear of failure, even if unconscious, can habitually make us take the safe path and limit us from realizing our full potential.

We are always given a choice in how to shape our lives. Fear does not have to go unchecked.

Courage is the antidote to fear. And courage is a muscle, which starts small, and needs exercise to grow strong. We can practice courage every day in the smallest ways. Talk to the people who intimidate you, until they don't. Cook a meal you've never cooked before and laugh if it's terrible. Learn a new sport or hobby and, when you fall, brush yourself off, get back up, and do it again. Become comfortable with being the perfectly imperfect human that you are, and experience a bigger, bolder, and more fulfilled life.

So, go ahead. Take the chance. Love deeply, hurt when you must, belly laugh, and soulfully cry. And when you feel the fear, smile knowingly, breathe deeply, and trust your training. You've got this.

—*Laura Dawn*

Life Wisdom:

— — — — — — — — — — — — — — — — —

— —

— — — — — — — — — — — — — — —

— — — — — — —

```
M  U  S  C  L  E  Y  R  Y  R  A  E  F  W
L  A  U  G  H  L  E  O  C  Y  R  C  E  C
A  N  C  Y  L  D  J  O  H  H  L  W  E  N
N  E  Q  E  L  Y  U  E  O  A  E  V  O  L
R  H  B  O  N  L  E  C  I  T  C  A  R  P
O  T  B  U  I  P  U  T  C  R  B  D  R  I
G  A  G  E  O  E  N  F  E  S  A  T  F  T
T  E  E  A  C  E  R  S  L  W  W  I  C  A
T  R  H  T  T  D  H  T  N  U  H  O  N  C
E  B  A  O  R  E  G  G  I  B  O  T  L  A
S  M  P  I  B  U  T  N  A  K  I  S  A  P
L  L  E  S  N  B  S  R  O  D  T  S  U  T
T  E  P  S  O  I  Y  T  O  R  F  C  R  I
O  S  M  I  L  E  N  T  U  P  T  R  A  V
C  O  U  R  A  G  E  G  A  G  S  S  E  E
```

Antidote	Cry	Muscle
Belly	Dawn	New
Bigger	Deeply	Potential
Bolder	Fear	Practice
Breathe	Heart	Smile
Captive	Hobby	Soulfully
Choice	Joy	Sport
Coin	Laugh	Strong
Cook	Laura	Training
Courage	Love	Trust

4   Renew Your Sense of Wonder

We are born full of wonder. As children we ask lots of questions. We are innocent and curious, wanting to understand. When we graduate school and college, we think we have all the knowledge we need to be successful. That's when we stop wondering.

At first, life is good, and we enjoy being competent. We achieve a lot and our resumes look great. As each day comes and goes, after a while it feels like our creativity runs dry. We start grieving on the inside, feeling like we are missing something. Something that gives life meaning.

We realize we are hungry for more depth and adventure. We want more inner peace and fulfillment. We've discovered that the things we can buy only bring joy for a moment.

When we stay awake to this deeper yearning, wonderful things start to happen. We open our hearts and minds to a much bigger universe. We reclaim our innocence and experience awe in even the smallest of happenings. We marvel at a sunset and are beguiled by the moon. We are amazed by the way the light dances on the water and how a caterpillar transforms into a butterfly. Our souls start singing. A sense of wonder reignites our being. We are fully alive again, this time from the inside out.

—*Sabina Spencer*

Life Wisdom:

__ __ __ __ __   __ __ __ __ __   __ __ __   __

__ __ __ __   __ __ __   __ __ __ __   __ __ __ __ __ __

__ __ __ __   __ __ __ __   __ __ __ __ __ __ __

```
T E U N I V E R S E N S E E M
H D W A T E R S R E N E W T M
G I B R S N A C E O E R E A E
I S W O E S E N O C A S R Y D
L N E R T L I M A L N V E A S
B I K R I E A E L U E A C D A
H U A I N S P I S L R L D V B
D E T A G N P D L N I I F E I
H E B T I R E E I C O F G N N
U E C N E C O N N I M U L T A
N E S T R R G H S C I E V U E
G R A Y O J F M T L E O R R F
R C E V I L A L E P U R E E M
Y R E D N O W D Y W E O A R V
E L G N I G N I S O A D S U S
```

Adventure	Hungry	Sabina
Alive	Innocence	Sense
Awe	Inside	Singing
Beguiled	Joy	Souls
Butterfly	Light	Spencer
Caterpillar	Marvel	Sunset
Dances	Moon	Universe
Depth	Peace	Water
Fulfillment	Reignites	Wonder
Hearts	Renew	Yearning

Family is the Best

The most important thing to me in life is family because I love them and they love me. We all protect each other and share and make each other laugh. Family always helps and supports me. They're always there if I need them.

They also buy me presents which makes me happy. I always like to make presents for Mommy and Daddy to show them how much I love them.

My favorite things to do with my family are play games, cuddle, cook, and talk about my day. My most favorite thing of anything I get to do with my family is giving a hundred thousand kisses and hugs!

They teach me lots of things, too. I always ask a million questions. If they don't know the answer, they always go find out so I can keep learning new stuff.

Family is the best and that's all.

—*Mckenzee Lee Kish*

Life Wisdom:

__ __ __ __ __   __ __   __ __ __   __ __ __ __   __ __ __ __ __

__ __   __ __ __   __ __ __ __ __

```
F A H C A E T K L A T K Q
E T I R O V A F I M I U I
E Y N L Y S I H S S E T P
Z P K A L A U G H S S H R
N P O H T N T P T E B E E
E A O E D R H I P B S L S
K H C R T R O T H O E P E
C T E I E N U P N Y R S N
M D C W S G S I M L N T T
T H S E L E A R N I N G S
E N E W T O N G A M E S H
A L O V E O D P L A Y G A
C U D D L E R L I F E U R
N O I L L I M P R L D H E
```

Answer	Hundred	Million
Best	Important	Play
Cook	Kish	Presents
Cuddle	Kisses	Protect
Family	Laugh	Questions
Favorite	Learning	Share
Games	Lee	Supports
Happy	Life	Talk
Helps	Love	Teach
Hugs	Mckenzee	Thousand

Music to the Rescue

Can music change a life? We sure think so. *Music to the rescue* is our motto and we live it every day.

We have created and sustained a home for vulnerable children called M-Lisada in the city of Kampala, the capital of Uganda, Africa. Music is at the center of all of our lives. All of our children learn an instrument, dance in the culture troupe, or train in acrobatics.

Though from different backgrounds, all are united. We each faced challenges early in our lives. Through music we have fun, learn teamwork, improve our study and social skills, and discover that we can bring joy to ourselves and others.

Our brass band has marched throughout Uganda while the culture group performs dances from every region. We play traditional instruments such as *adungu*, *akogo*, and *amadinda*. The acrobats amaze audiences with their abilities.

Our home was started in 1996 by an orphaned twelve-year-old boy who had two dreams: he wanted to perform for appreciative audiences, and to care for his three younger sisters. He soon banded together with a handful of other kids living in the slums of Katwe.

Since that time, over one thousand children have lived at or received training from M-Lisada. Several have graduated secondary school, and some have even gone on to university, law school, and nursing school. Others have become professional musicians and music teachers throughout East Africa.

Music has changed so many lives. How has it enhanced yours?

—*Chris Weigers*

Life Wisdom:

___ ___ ___   ___ ___ ___   ___ ___ ___ ___   ___ ___

___ ___ ___   ___ ___   ___ ___   ___ ___ ___ ___   ___ ___ ___

___ ___ ___   ___ ___ ___   ___ ___ ___ ___   ___ ___ ___ ___

```
A  M  A  D  I  N  D  A  S  E  E  M  U  S  I
D  D  A  N  C  E  N  E  S  R  R  M  C  F  R
U  T  E  E  S  U  C  R  E  S  E  A  O  A  V
N  S  N  E  F  N  R  U  Y  O  A  G  C  H  N
G  E  D  E  E  W  M  T  H  A  F  R  I  C  A
U  O  P  I  M  L  A  L  Y  S  O  I  B  E  T
T  O  D  B  K  U  E  U  I  B  J  C  O  A  W
M  U  N  E  M  O  R  C  A  S  A  O  R  B  U
A  R  E  S  C  U  E  T  C  K  A  N  Y  I  N
E  T  R  E  H  A  I  H  S  L  O  D  D  L  I
N  C  D  W  T  C  O  I  A  N  H  G  A  I  T
E  I  L  T  S  O  R  P  Y  C  I  O  O  T  E
U  S  I  A  L  H  M  R  O  F  R  E  P  I  D
L  U  H  K  C  A  A  D  N  A  G  U  D  E  B
E  M  C  F  K  O  S  M  A  E  R  D  R  S  E
```

Abilities	Children	Katwe
Acrobatics	Chris	Kids
Adungu	Culture	Mlisada
Africa	Dance	Music
Akogo	Dreams	Perform
Amadinda	Fun	Rescue
Audiences	Home	School
Band	Instrument	Uganda
Brass	Joy	United
Care	Kampala	Weigers

Humor Me

Did you know that there are over twenty forms of humor? Humor has the power to bring about happiness and healing. It can also invoke or increase alienation, hurt, sadness, or depression.

Good humor brings laughter, smiles, eases tension, dissipates sadness, lightens the load, lifts spirits, and creates connection. It can also help heal a broken heart. Humor is a natural mood elevator and releases the feel-good chemical serotonin into the brain. When laughter flows freely and in good taste, energy follows and can actually improve health.

Humor can shift the energetic vibration of an entire room. It helps remove communication barriers of shyness and social awkwardness by breaking the ice. This is why so many speakers open up with a joke. One's sense of humor is developed by socio-cultural background, primary type of intelligence, and personality. As the legendary TV chef Julia Child says, "Nothing can alienate you faster than a sense of humor that doesn't gel with those around you." In other words, knowing your audience is key.

Dark or negatively used humor can weave a path of mental and emotional trauma. Avoid it. If it hurts or shames or makes fun of another, even ourselves, it's not really funny. Being the butt of a joke, whether cultural or personal, feels terrible.

Use humor and laughter to enhance life. Keep it light and keep it happy. Most importantly, bring on the smiles!

—*Frankie Merrill*

Life Wisdom:

— — — — — — — — — — — — — — — —

— — — — — — — — — — — — — — — — — — — — —

— — — — — — — — — — — — — — — — — — —

— — — — —

```
U T H S E H L R O M U H U M O
R A A T R O T A V E L E G O B
F S P R I P E N U Y E K N G L
R T P A O N E F U G G H I T E
A E Y W H N L R A N H D L C O
N N E A E O O V C N E T A S C
K R N R W L L I R R E M E T L
I C G S I O T B T L J L H R A
E Y N A P E N R D C I O T O C
Y L I G G I H A T M E G K U I
T L P R N G R T S A R N H E M
O R E I O M O I M O O D N T E
O N A E S E R O T O N I N O H
E R C E R R A N D S E N S E C
B I L I H F F E I M P R O V E
```

Brain	Good	Light
Chemical	Happy	Merrill
Connection	Healing	Mood
Elevator	Heart	Power
Energetic	Humor	Sense
Energy	Ice	Serotonin
Enhance	Improve	Smiles
Flows	Joke	Spirits
Frankie	Key	Taste
Freely	Laughter	Vibration

Pirate Wisdom

Ahoy Mates, all hands-on deck! Raise your sails and prepare for every adventure. We're hitting the high seas and it's important to navigate carefully through the waves of life. Check your map and lay in your course, for there are many obstacles on the voyage. Small corrections have big impact, so be mindful of the trim of your sails. When conditions allow, make merry and bring on the music, for tomorrow the winds may change.

As the captain of your own ship (and a fine vessel it is), know that your decisions affect all on board. The crew, the passengers, the cargo, and the ship herself all depend on you. Batten down the hatches and sail a true course to happiness. Show glee when you can. Those around you need to see the example.

Treasure! Ahh, "X" marks the spot. Find your treasure wherever you are filled with joy. There is plenty of booty to go around. Remember that the greatest treasure of all is love. Even the captain gets a kiss.

Drink your grog of life right down to the dregs! Then fill it back up and do it again! Sail far and fast, with the wind at your back. Enjoy moments of calm seas and smooth sailing. Avoid the sea monsters as best you can. Steer carefully through the shallow shoals of life and take pleasure in your companions. Laugh long, laugh loud, and laugh often. Yo ho ho!

Look to the horizon and follow the stars. Know that your guiding star will always lead you home.

As you were, Mates.

— *Pirate Captain Loren Smith*

Life Wisdom:

___ ___ ___ ___ ___ ___   ___ ___ ___ ___ ___ ___   ___   ___ ___ ___ ___

___ ___   ___ ___ ___ ___ ___ ___   ___   ___ ___ ___

___ ___ ___ ___ ___ ___ ___   ___ ___ ___   ___ ___   ___ ___ ___ ___ ___

___ ___ ___   ___ ___ ___

```
C C W S E V A W S R A T S H
E R A S R E T S N O M P A M
K T E R H E E E M R S A E H
I I L W G N V I N O G A T T
S P S H I O I P O R D C A I
S L E P L D R C I V O S G M
I E P R N G V M A M A C I S
A A R W U O A H P P E R V W
H S L E Y T V A E R T Y A O
U U G A E N N O L T H A N E
R R G S U I E E E T A R I P
E E E S O G S R V D E C K N
Y A H N L S H O O D R E G S
U I S E E G R O G L A H O Y
P A E V T R E A S U R E R E
```

Adventure	Happiness	Pleasure
Ahoy	Kiss	Sea
Captain	Laugh	Ship
Cargo	Loren	Smith
Companions	Love	Star
Crew	Map	Treasure
Deck	Mates	Vessel
Dregs	Monsters	Voyage
Glee	Navigate	Waves
Grog	Pirate	Wisdom

9   **The Love of My Life**

The most important thing that ever happened to me was meeting the love of my life, my wife Jill. I was a professional captain on large yachts. Relationships were always a hit-and-miss situation because of the nature of my work. I was gone for long stretches and had no time for a long-term relationship.

When I least expected it, something wonderful happened. In 1995, I stopped in Cabo San Lucas, Mexico on my way to Costa Rica to deliver a large sailboat to its owner. We joined some people visiting from Arizona for dinner. That's when I met her.

Jill and I saw each other a few times in a group. The day we sailed, she delivered the best chili I have ever had, enough for a week at sea. At that point I offered a meeting in the near future!

We eventually rendezvoused in San Diego, California, where I lived aboard my forty-foot sailboat. We became good friends. I helped her start a new vocation as a chef. Jill joined my crew in the San Diego Schooner Cup race. That evening, we got together and that's all it took. I invited Jill to come live with me on my boat. Happily, she did.

We knew, at first meeting, that we were soul mates and best friends. For twenty-five years we have been inseparable. We lived on my sailboat (no easy task) for fifteen years. Jill became an award-winning chef. We worked together on large motor yachts until we retired. We married on 05/05/05 in Emerald Bay, Lake Tahoe. For me, there is nothing in this world better than having my forever relationship with Jill.

—*Captain Dennis Daoust*

Life Wisdom:

_ _ _ _   _ _ _ _   _ _ _ _ _ _   _ _ _ _ _ _ _   _ _

_ _ _ _   _ _ _ _   _ _ _ _ _ _ _   _ _

_ _ _ _ _ _ _ _ _ _ _   _ _ _ _ _   _ _   _ _ _ _

_ _ _   _ _   _ _ _ _ _ _

```
W H E A B A Y S Y L I P P A H
N Y O R S E A M C S U E V O L
L F R I E N D N E H O E A D E
S J B Z T E O S W X O U X L O
P I O O E I E C T E I O L A H
T L A N T L I T R H R C N R A
R L T A L I B E F E C C O E T
C E C A N E V A C H O A A M R
N O T G F E E I R S R N Y E M
V D E I R R A M T A C W O A D
C E L O R N D A C H P E T A R
H N F F U E R E E L W E O A Y
I N S I F I D F Y O S U S U L
L I E T C L A K E I S T H N A
I S P A P E C A P T A I N N I
```

Arizona	Emerald	Mates
Bay	Forever	Mexico
Boat	Friend	Race
Captain	Happily	Retired
Chef	Inseparable	Schooner
Chili	Jill	Sea
Costa Rica	Lake	Soul
Crew	Life	Tahoe
Daoust	Love	Vocation
Dennis	Married	Yachts

10   Happiness is Contagious

Did you know you can catch happiness from your friends? It's true. And likewise, you can spread your happiness to them. Social networking research has shown that the people in our lives are incredibly influential. This isn't just a matter of "birds of a feather flock together," but rather contagion, whether positive or negative.

We influence those around us, just as those around us influence us. Happiness is contagious. When we choose to smile at someone, whether a loved one or a stranger, we are influencing the great web of human connectivity.

We tend to think of ourselves as individually separate, as though we are a single being independent of our environment. In truth, we are interwoven into the fabric of existence. A single smile or act of goodwill reverberates through the chain of being, increasing overall happiness. Conversely, negative expressions and behaviors are also contagious.

Be mindful of your influence on the delicate web of human coexistence. Be aware of those with whom you choose to associate. Is your circle full of love and support? If not, what words and actions can you make go viral to generate more positivity within your community?

Choose to spread happiness. Be joyously contagious. Be grateful for those who reciprocate happiness to you. Let's make happiness go viral in our world.

—John Hood

Life Wisdom:

___ ___ _ _____

___ _____ __

_____ __ ___ _____

____ __ _____

```
Y O E T A C I L E D F L O C K
U A C R E D A T T R U A N S M
S D R O W I A T R F T H E R A
N S B F N R D E E O R A E C S
E I D E E T J T R N P P V D E
R O F N W A A O H P O P R A P
P I E E E R T G Y S S I U N E
M G C V G I O H I O B N T S S
I C I O S V R T E O U E I C N
N I R W E T I F H R U S E G A
D R B R L V I R A L H S L R E
F C A E I N F L U E N C E Y A
U L F T M T C H A I V H T N O
L E Y N S D O O H F B O O A E
L L L I W D O O G I N G L J C
```

Action	Full	Love
Birds	Generate	Mindful
Catch	Goodwill	Overall
Circle	Grateful	Positivity
Contagious	Happiness	Smile
Delicate	Hood	Spread
Fabric	Influence	Support
Feather	Interwoven	Viral
Flock	John	Web
Friends	Joyously	Words

The Pursuit of Happiness

Are you happy? What does that even mean? The outside world tells us that being happy is one of life's ultimate goals. Is it one of yours?

The definition of happiness can be a slippery slope. It means different things to different people. The world seems to be obsessed with the pursuit of happiness. Philosophers, theologians, psychologists, and even economists have long sought to define and measure it. Many talk about it like it's the flavor of the month. "Would you like a scoop of cookies 'n cream?"

"Life, Liberty and the *pursuit* of Happiness" is a well-known phrase in the United States Declaration of Independence. The phrase gives three examples of the "unalienable Rights" which the Declaration says have been given to all humans by their Creator, and which governments are created to protect. That means we have the right to *pursue*, but *getting* happiness is not guaranteed.

Pursuing happiness is like pursuing a mate: it's all about the chase. Chases are only fun when in-process. What do we do if we catch it? Maybe catching it isn't the point. Maybe we can stop *pursuing* happiness and allow it to come into our lives.

We've experienced both happiness and sorrow. Happiness seems fleeting, while sorrow seems to linger. Loss imbues life with depth. Happiness is the fun sparkly stuff that runs around the edges and brings moments of delight. It's like a butterfly—beautiful, flitting, ephemeral, and then gone.

When every day and every thought is centered around what we think will make us happy, the pursuit of happiness can become an expensive, time-consuming, and exhausting addiction with us looking for our next fix. One way we can get a clue that we're on the happiness pursuit merry-go-round is if we are constantly saying and thinking things like, *I am happy but....* Danger! Be careful! We could let our big *but* get in the way of our happiness!

Many of us have done what has been necessary to create good lives for our families, our communities, our country, and ourselves. Did doing that make us *happy*? Mostly not, particularly at the time we were doing those things. However, all of the sacrifices, selfless service, and postponed satisfaction have helped us realize that the ultimate place of inner peace is the quiet joy of contentment.

Contentment allows us to find happiness in wanting what we have and appreciating what we've done to get it. We may not be happy with all of the aches, pains, and challenges of our bodies. We can be content with the fact that it beats the alternative. Happy is for the moment. Contentment is for the long term. Happiness is our inner child and contentment is our inner sage. Have a happy birthday and a contented life.

Being contented and happy does not mean settling. Quite the opposite. It helps keep our emotions on an even keel and reduces the drama and stress in our lives. Contentment is a firm foundation. We can always improve. When we take stock of our lives right now, we honor all that has brought us to this point. Then we use that as our launch pad to grow, expand, and progress. We are able to focus on what we *can* do, not what we can't. Even the smallest changes will bring us to new levels of happiness in the moment and ongoing contentment in the long run.

This doesn't mean we can't have goals for a better or different lifestyle. It's important to find acceptance and contentment no matter what. Even if we have no material wealth, we can enjoy a sunrise. Even if we feel alone, we can partake in a conversation with a stranger. Even if our health is challenged, we can experience moments of joy.

Look around, breathe, listen. Dig into your heart for something to be grateful for. Focus your full attention on it. Feel the joy, peace, and sense of fulfillment. This is contentment. Notice if you have it, or even the beginning elements from which to create it. Embrace it. Enjoy it.

Pursue happiness all you wish. Know that it's an ephemeral butterfly that can crush us in the attempt to capture it or be enjoyed immensely in all its fleeting glory. Cultivate contentment. Don't worry. Be happy.

Cultivate Happiness and Joy

What makes us happy? It could be dining with a dear friend. Or scoring that new pair of shoes, especially on sale! Maybe conquering a piano piece, or a difficult crossword, or a commendation by the boss, or taking a great vacation, or enjoying a great book. The point is we feel happy when we accomplish something we want. Our sense of self-worth is amplified. Happiness makes our egos feel good.

Happiness is different than joy. We feel happy when things go our way. Joy speaks to the heart and happens when we connect to the wonder of the Universe. Joy is all around us when we take time to notice. It's always available. It could be stopping to appreciate the beauty of a bud opening into a glorious flower, or the miracle of an acorn becoming a great oak, or the wonder of cloud formations, or the purring of a cat. We can be overcome with grief at losing a loved one and still feel joy watching a puppy frolic in the grass. Joy feeds the soul. Happiness feeds the ego.

We need both. We are groomed to seek happiness through accumulating, whether it's things, material wealth, achievements, or even education. These things matter. There are things that matter even more, and they are not things. True value and deep satisfaction arise from within. This is the experience of joy.

—*Susan Sokol Blosser*

Life Wisdom:

_ _ _ _   _ _ _ _   _ _ _ _   _ _ _ _   _ _   _ _ _ _ _

_ _ _ _   _ _ _ _   _ _ _ _ _ _   _ _   _ _ _ _ _ _

_ _ _ _ _ _ _ _ _ _

```
L  O  W  O  K  F  D  V  P  U  R  R  I  N  G
R  E  W  O  L  F  A  R  W  J  B  L  T  Y  R
S  O  R  T  N  C  H  E  O  O  E  U  R  T  E
J  A  O  Y  A  D  A  Y  O  W  I  O  A  U  S
N  Y  T  T  O  L  E  K  U  R  S  S  E  A  S
L  I  I  I  T  F  G  R  A  S  S  S  H  E  O
G  O  G  H  S  C  O  N  N  E  C  T  O  B  L
N  R  L  C  E  F  A  N  N  D  W  E  R  B
A  F  O  L  T  C  A  I  H  I  I  L  T  S  C
P  R  R  O  A  P  P  C  E  P  C  H  H  E  A
I  O  I  U  M  P  R  U  T  A  L  O  T  E  V
A  L  O  D  A  E  L  E  R  I  E  O  K  I  R
N  I  U  H  Y  A  D  I  W  S  O  H  K  A  W
O  C  S  E  V  R  M  S  U  S  A  N  E  O  O
Y  P  P  U  P  N  O  I  T  A  C  U  D  E  S
```

Beauty	Grass	Satisfaction
Blosser	Groomed	Shoes
Book	Happiness	Sokol
Cloud	Heart	Soul
Connect	Joy	Susan
Crossword	Miracle	Vacation
Education	Oak	Value
Flower	Piano	Wealth
Frolic	Puppy	Within
Glorious	Purring	Wonder

Find Joy

We all want more joy in our lives. The trick is in knowing how and where to find it. Our complex human lifestyles are tangled up with obligations, distractions, and alluring technology. These complications can lead us to yearn for simplicity, and for a chance to smile more and worry less.

Unlike humans, savoring moments of joy comes easily to most animals. They can be great teachers for us in many ways. Whether it is napping in a sunbeam or running for the sheer joy of it, animals have a knack for finding happiness and basking in joy. Their winning formula seems to center around an acceptance for what is. They don't label or judge what should be or might have been. Free from the burden of evaluating everything that happens, animals joyfully leap, hop, dash, snooze, and munch their way through life.

Take a hint from the animals' approach to life. Let go of past regrets and future expectations. We too can allow ourselves to fully experience the potential that each moment has to offer us. Increase the feeling of happiness in life by letting go of judgement and labels. Open your heart to the flowering of joy. Let our animal companions and the beauty of nature lead the way. They know how to find and experience joy every day.

—*Lauren McCall*

Life Wisdom:

__ __ __ __ __ __ __ __ __ __ __ __ __ __ __ __ __ __ __

__ __ __ __ __ __ __ __ __ __ __ __ __ __ __ __ __ __

__ __ __ __ __ __ __ __ __ __ __ __

```
A P O T E N T I A L E A P N I
F M A Y Y L G G H I N T S T E
O S L A O T N C N A T U R E H
R N A G H J I C U I G S H O A
M O U N W T R C O N N L A C P
U O R I F E E L I N G N C I P
L Z E K A V W R E L I E I F I
A E N S U L O L Y M P M A W N
N D E A N V L D A T C M J O E
B A A B A Y F L A C F U I L S
K E P S N O I N A P M O C S S
F N A P H L C L H C N U M Y W
I R A U I E L T W O L L A H O
U T E C T N R T R A E H O P E
G R E E K Y G M A E B N U S T
```

Acceptance	Free	McCall
Allow	Happiness	Munch
Animal	Heart	Napping
Basking	Hint	Nature
Beauty	Hop	Potential
Companions	Increase	Savoring
Dash	Joy	Simplicity
Feeling	Knack	Snooze
Flowering	Lauren	Sunbeam
Formula	Leap	Winning

Commune with Nature

The innate, intelligent communication systems that exist among plants, trees, animals, pets, and nature are already scientifically proven. Communication networks exist within, and between, the species as a sort of *mind-meld*. I like to refer to it as *communing*. Communing with each other is a vital and necessary component of the living world, and is paramount to species' survival on Earth.

The relationships between animals, nature, and humans are the topic of many films. Movies depict themes showing interspecies friendships and cohabitation, warring and survival, respect, perseverance, and love. Those that feature different species communing and partnering on a journey together ending with love, survival, and ultimately triumph are usually the most successful.

We watch brilliant screen stories with species seeking to find answers to their extinction. As humans, we seem to have lost our way as it relates to natural survival. Communing and gaining a vital information flow to assist each other could be the missing key to ensuring our future.

Connect with other species. Commune with nature. Enhance your life. Be a part of the solution. Your actions make a difference. Together, we can save the world.

—*Eileen Kurlander*

Life Wisdom:

_ __ __ __ __ __ __ __   __ __ __   __ __ __

_ __ __ __ __ __ __ __   __ __ __ __   __ __ __ __ __

__ __   __ __ __   __ __   __ __ __   __ __ __ __ __ __

```
C O F S T E P C R E S P E C T
Y E N R U O J M O R E A R T H
S L M U I F N I E M S M L I F
C T A N N E U D H P M U I R T
R S N T G A N T N A M U H W I
E A L A I A T D U T H A N N L
E V N A L V C U S R D A S E A
N E S R M P E S R H E M E V V
H O U S I I N S T E I I E O I
A K I N G O N E A N L P R R V
N R T T I H O A D O E S T P R
C P E T U C C M V I E E S I U
E S C Y K L E E E Y N T O O S
U A E R S L O S P E C I E S U
R K V I D V A S M O V I E S L
```

Actions	Human	Proven
Animals	Journey	Respect
Commune	Key	Save
Connect	Kurlander	Screen
Earth	Love	Solution
Eileen	Mind Meld	Species
Enhance	Movies	Survival
Films	Nature	Trees
Friendship	Pets	Triumph
Future	Plants	Vital

14   Seek Sanctuary in Nature

Most of us crave sanctuary, a refuge from the business of life; a sacred place. Many have lost sight of what our ancestors innately knew: that beautiful Mother Earth gives birth to us, nurtures us, and sustains all life. We are no longer taught to respect nature, nor to know that nature is the giver of life. We are taught to be consumers, that there isn't enough for everyone, and that we, ourselves, are not enough.

We are part of nature, yet we feel separated from her. We feel like she's over there, and we're over here.

The sanctuary we seek is all around us. It is the natural environment. We've gotten so busy and caught up that we often ignore her. We belong with nature, with our fingers in the soil and our noses in blossoms. Spending time in nature allows us to experience the wonderment of our existence with all our senses. Nature allows us to shift our attention beyond the busyness of our lives. We can recognize that we are inextricably connected to the Universe.

Spend time in nature. Venture into the woods, the desert, the ocean, or a lake. Go sit on a rock. Return to Mother. Create your own sanctuary. Make a refuge. It will be yours to share with everyone. There is enough. We are not separate. We are one. One flower. One Earth.

—*John Beaudry*

Life Wisdom:

___ ___ ___ ___ ___   ___ ___ ___ ___ ___   ___ ___ ___   ___ ___ ___ ___ ___

___ ___ ___ ___ ___   ___ ___   ___ ___ ___ ___ ___ ___   ___ ___ ___

```
R  N  U  O  W  F  L  O  W  E  R  R  S  T
Y  E  N  U  W  O  O  D  S  R  E  A  U  S
R  E  S  N  S  N  N  E  O  S  N  A  S  E
D  T  U  P  H  M  T  D  R  C  R  E  T  S
U  M  S  O  E  A  O  E  E  C  E  A  A  N
A  O  J  E  E  C  G  S  R  R  Y  A  I  E
E  T  N  R  S  N  T  A  S  R  M  D  N  S
B  H  C  A  I  O  V  L  A  O  L  E  S  O
S  E  L  F  R  E  N  U  E  E  L  W  N  N
A  R  I  S  A  N  T  T  U  G  K  B  R  T
C  A  O  E  A  C  K  C  O  R  U  A  T  O
R  H  S  T  N  N  H  T  R  I  B  F  L  U
E  S  U  A  R  T  U  E  R  U  T  N  E  V
D  R  S  R  E  Y  T  R  E  S  E  D  O  R
E  A  R  T  H  U  N  I·V  E  R  S  E  U
```

Ancestors	John	Sacred
Beaudry	Lake	Sanctuary
Birth	Mother	Senses
Blossoms	Nature	Share
Crave	Noses	Soil
Create	Ocean	Sustains
Desert	One	Universe
Earth	Refuge	Venture
Fingers	Respect	Wonderment
Flower	Rock	Woods

The Gift of Patience

There are an abundance of distractions and external stimulation that compete for our time and attention. The gift of patience is becoming a rare legacy in today's world. The evolution of our humanity requires a slow and steady, persevering, and flexible pace.

As humans, the heart of our capacity to live is fulfilled through our journey in life. It's the way we know we are alive and how we measure our success.

Nature shows us that, like a seed that has been planted, the germination process happens gradually when the conditions are right. The soil temperature, the amount of water, and sunlight all have to be in perfect harmony for the seed to sprout. When we slow down and embrace patience for the gift it is, we are able to dive deep. We allow our journey to guide us knowing that when the conditions are harmonized we will receive clarity about what steps to take and when. We eliminate obstacles and speed our progress.

There are many simple yet powerful ways to use patience to enjoy our passage through life. Lie on the grass in a park and gaze up at the clouds as they slowly float by and observe the continual changing forms that take shape. Sit next to a river and reflect on how the rushing waters flow in and out of the slow-moving pools on the river's edge. Sleep on an important decision rather than make an immediate choice.

Notice how slowing down improves progress and provides peace, joy, and gratitude. Feel the quiet adventure of patience.

—*Teresa Helgeson*

Life Wisdom:

___ ___ ___   ___ ___ ___   ___ ___ ___ ___   ___ ___ ___ ___   ___ ___ ___ ___

___ ___ ___   ___ ___ ___ ___ ___ ___   ___ ___ ___ ___ ___ ___   ___ ___ ___

___ ___ ___ ___ ___   ___ ___ ___ ___ ___

```
C S F W H E P P O B S E R V E
L H L J N Y A R O U H S L Y E
O A O O O T W Y O A O U O R E
U P W G I U R P R G A J U C T
D E I E C E R M Y O R T A A U
S F N N A C O N H I N E O E T
T C V O E N E M E E P L S C O
E M E S Y D N T V Y F R E S E
U S P E T M U D A N E L D S M
Y L E G A U A T D V F G I L B
D O E L R S O K I E P E V O R
A O L E A T E R R T D E E W A
E P S H E R S R P A A E E U C
T C L E G A C Y E S P R E D E
S Y T I R A L C C T E S G S S
```

Adventure	Harmony	Progress
Clarity	Helgeson	Reflect
Clouds	Journey	River
Deep	Joy	Seed
Dive	Legacy	Shape
Embrace	Observe	Sleep
Float	Park	Slow
Flow	Patience	Sprout
Gift	Peace	Steady
Gratitude	Pools	Teresa

16   Relaxation Is Creativity

Tension is who you think you should be. Relaxation is who you are.
—*Chinese Proverb*

It is easy to forget the magic of slowing down. In such a fast-paced world, we can get tied up in things that we think we *should* be doing instead of things we *could* be doing. For many people, relaxation is viewed as less of a must-do and more of a luxury enjoyment that we can indulge in from time to time.

Though seldom talked about, there is a hidden dimension of creativity to relaxation. Think about relaxation in terms of letting go of energy. This gives us a framework for imagining how new energy can enter in to take the place of the old. That is the creativity hidden in relaxation.

We need to use our imaginations. A real process takes place on the level of subtle energy. Any time we let go of an old commitment, idea, or project, we free up brain bandwidth to take on something new. Even if we do not know for sure what is coming next, we will have at least created some energetic space. There's a place for the new to inhabit when it does finally begin to take shape.

Remember that, by letting go, we can always create space. We can gain a deeper creative strength. We can open up more room in our lives, minds, and hearts to pursue that which matters to us the most.

—*Dylan Field*

Life Wisdom:

__ __ __ __ __ __ __ __ __ __ __ __ __ __ __ __

__ __ __ __ __ __ __ __ __ __ __

__ __ __ __ __ __ __ __ __ __ __ __ __

```
H I D D E N R M A G I C D L O
B E E L D L E I F L U X U R Y
R A X U H T G N E R T S Y O A
E E T I S O N N A L Y D G O A
V H L S T R A E H L C L R M O
O I T A W S U U P R O C E S S
R N S D X S T P E O O N N P B
P D D E I A N A O G O U E R R
M U N E I W T N N I D S A A I
S L I N E I D I S D H I E N S
U G M A V P W N O R N T H E E
B E S I T O E O A N O A V C P
T U T R L M O R W B B I A N A
L Y N S I A E D I I L P W E H
E I S D N E X T T D S O M W S
```

Bandwidth	Idea	Process
Brain	Indulge	Proverb
Creativity	Inhabit	Pursue
Deeper	Lives	Relaxation
Dimension	Luxury	Room
Dylan	Magic	Shape
Energy	Minds	Slowing
Field	New	Space
Hearts	Next	Strength
Hidden	Old	Subtle

Find Your Why

Our planet works on the simple premise of seed, cultivate, and harvest. What do you want to grow? What kind of magic in your life do you want to create? Why?

People often find doing this meditation gives them a starting point for planting the seed of a life they love.

Close your eyes. Get yourself centered with your feet planted on the ground or floor. Breathe in through your nose, all the way down past your lungs to your roots. Exhale from your mouth. Repeat three times.

Think about what you would do, if anything in the world were available to you. What would fill your soul? Where would you live? What would you do, be, and have?

Often while doing this exercise, it is easy to think about all the things we do not want, rather than what we do. Remove all the yak-yak of belief. Ignore what you have been told about the possibilities. Most importantly, consider *why* you are doing what you are doing. Let the information flow. Write it down.

Reflect on what you believe about yourself. Trust yourself. You have in you what the stars are made of. You are a star with the ability to manifest anything you desire.

Choose wisely and well.

—*Lynne Hardin*

Life Wisdom:

— — —   — —   — —   — — —   — — — — —   — —

— — — —   — — — —   — — —   — — —   — — — — —

—   — — — — —   — — —   — — — —

```
Y L E S I W E L E W O R G
S E Y E T G A R D L R O W
C O O S N B K F I O L T T
D U T F I N A I D S S S H
E A L L A S Y T O U E S A
R O I T F I K L R F T D R
W T N D I Y A T I O O U V
Y M N R W V Y N O H Y A E
F M A O N H A R D I N D S
E L O G S M C T R D L S T
I T L U I E E A E U G T E
L E A I T C A E O N L F U
E Y V E F H S S U L T U R
B E H O R E F L E C T Y O
U L O W L C V W F E E T E
```

Ability	Hardin	Roots
Belief	Harvest	Seed
Create	Love	Soul
Cultivate	Lungs	Star
Desire	Lynne	Trust
Eyes	Magic	Well
Feet	Manifest	Why
Fill	Mouth	Wisely
Flow	Nose	World
Grow	Reflect	Yak Yak

Sacred Soul Purpose

Life does not come with an instruction manual. It comes with free will and an inner knowing that we have a sacred soul purpose. Our mission is to find it.

What is your sacred soul purpose? You may have already discovered it and be pursuing it daily. It's a feeling of *just right*. When we finally feel at home and have a sense of soul-deep fulfilment, we're there. It can be difficult to find that sacred path. We start by following our dreams.

This urge to live our dreams takes us to our sacred calling. Follow it! Grow, shift the inner world. Give birth to your soul's calling, let spirit come through. Transmute. Transcend. Transform. It's not a one-size-fits-all experience. It's an individual, spirit-guided, and soul-led journey.

Sometimes the path to light is through the dark. The dark night of the soul is a common spiritual experience. After the eclipse, the light returns. We emerge with a new sparkle, resilience, and resolve.

One's sacred soul purpose may not be in what we pursue professionally. Or it might. This is an individual arena that each has to answer for themselves. Many people find solace in solitude. The outside world doesn't always help.

Our souls have a longing. When we follow that longing, we can be led to our individual sacred soul purpose. We can definitely achieve it. Let Divine Spirit lead you on this serendipitous path of continuous growth to true fulfilment. The pursuit brings the deepest joy imaginable.

—*Lydia Proschinger*

Life Wisdom:

———— ——— —— —— ————— ———
————— ———— —— ———— -
——————————— ————— ——
——— —————

```
P  T  D  I  V  I  N  E  P  E  A  C  S  H  A
G  R  O  W  T  H  D  D  L  U  O  E  N  E  C
O  A  O  F  U  U  E  Y  E  N  R  U  O  J  H
S  N  W  S  T  R  D  A  D  E  E  P  L  K  I
S  S  O  I  C  I  T  R  N  E  T  R  O  U  E
N  F  L  A  A  H  E  D  R  R  U  E  S  S  V
A  O  S  C  G  A  I  R  E  F  M  N  D  P  E
S  R  I  I  M  P  D  N  E  C  S  N  A  R  T
A  M  L  S  I  T  T  S  G  H  N  I  P  T  O
S  E  J  T  S  I  P  S  P  E  A  U  L  F  R
E  O  O  O  R  I  O  S  P  A  R  K  L  E  A
Y  U  U  I  L  L  M  L  W  S  T  I  Z  A  T
S  L  P  C  A  L  I  I  U  O  N  H  G  U  I
D  S  E  C  A  L  L  I  N  G  E  D  B  Y  O
U  R  E  W  S  L  T  D  A  R  K  O  U  L  S
```

Achieve	Joy	Serendipitous
Calling	Law	Solace
Dark	Light	Solitude
Divine	Lydia	Soul
Dreams	Mission	Sparkle
Eclipse	Path	Spirit
Free	Proschinger	Transcend
Growth	Purpose	Transform
Inner	Pursuit	Transmute
Journey	Sacred	Will

The Butterfly Spark

The fluttering path of the butterfly reminds me of the journey through life. With a beautiful variety of colors, they fly free. Before becoming a butterfly, the caterpillar has to change; its death is a spark to new life.

During our lives we can run into difficult situations that end up changing our direction. Life as we know it ends. It is a death of sorts. To go forward, we usually have to leave something behind.

When such times occur, we are always ready, even with the doubts that overwhelm the mind. We are always equipped to handle it.

Often after getting through the challenge, instead of taking one step ahead, we leap forward on the life path as our vibration rises. The harder the situation, the more progress it can bring. The old must be let go of, like a tree sheds its leaves.

Difficult conditions and demanding circumstances can bring positive growth. We can look at anything as negative, or even bad luck. However, we have the choice to remain positive as these troubling pockets in time pass. By embracing these opportunities that bring bright lessons to learn and grow from, the transition ahead becomes easier.

Like the butterfly, we end up with new and beautiful colors and take flight, continuing on as we savor life's nectar.

—Laron G.S.

Life Wisdom:

__ __ __ __ ___ ___ __ __ __ __ __ __ __ __

__ __ __ __ __ __ __ __ __ __ __ __ __ __ __ __ __ __ __

__ __ __ __ __ __ __ __ __

```
W  S  B  U  T  T  E  R  F  L  Y  I  T  N  E
W  R  E  G  R  O  W  T  H  N  H  O  E  E  U
T  E  A  V  L  E  S  S  O  N  S  G  R  T  H
E  S  N  L  A  P  E  I  D  E  A  T  H  A  P
N  R  A  E  L  E  T  V  R  T  L  K  O  F  O
V  M  T  H  G  I  L  F  I  C  U  H  B  F  C
I  P  I  A  S  D  P  V  R  T  F  R  L  R  K
B  L  R  N  N  R  E  R  Y  A  I  U  G  E  E
R  A  A  O  D  A  E  E  E  G  T  S  T  E  T
A  R  H  E  G  W  N  S  H  T  U  C  O  R  S
T  O  E  W  R  R  R  T  E  O  A  H  E  P  U
I  N  L  O  U  O  E  R  D  B  E  C  T  N  E
O  N  V  O  L  F  I  S  O  B  B  U  T  A  T
N  A  J  O  E  N  R  F  S  K  R  A  P  S  P
S  L  C  E  G  N  E  L  L  A  H  C  I  E  S
```

Beautiful	Free	New
Bright	Growth	Path
Butterfly	Journey	Pockets
Caterpillar	Laron	Positive
Challenge	Learn	Progress
Colors	Leaves	Savor
Death	Lessons	Spark
Flight	Mind	Transition
Fluttering	Nectar	Tree
Forward	Negative	Vibration

20   The Mighty Owl Butterfly

After being disillusioned by a religious practice that no longer served me, I lost my connection to a higher power. Life felt random. I wondered if I was as meaningless as a grain of sand on an endless beach.

A few years passed. One cold winter morning after a huge snowfall had cleared away the clouds, I drove out of my neighborhood. At the first stop sign, my eyes landed on a magnificent pine tree, heavy with snow, sparkling in the sunlight of the clear blue sky. In that instant, my breath was whisked away. I was overcome by a long-forgotten sense of awe and connection.

Shortly after, I happened upon a show about camouflage in nature. It struck me how perfectly some creatures blend into their surroundings. These incredible adaptations were viewed as *natural selection* and *accidental artifacts of pattern formation*. I couldn't wrap my brain around how such majesty could be accidental. I saw an owl butterfly with a perfect replica of an owl's eye on its wing. I knew with my whole being that was not *random*.

My shut-down spiritual heart was blasted open. Everywhere I looked I saw infinite intelligence, Divinity, and connection. I sensed a much bigger picture than my three-dimensional, five-sensory human life. It was there all along. I just needed to see. The context of my own existence had been completely expanded. Now even that grain of sand is meaningful and magnificent!

—Maryann Sperry

Life Wisdom:

__ __ __ __ __ __ __ __   __ __ __ __   __ __ __ __ __

__ __ __ __   __ __ __ __ __ __   __ __ __ __

__ __ __ __ __ __ __ __

```
R L A U T I R I P S I E F L E
C T R A E H A T I N E B N D N
G D N A S U N C F N E E B E N
Y T S E J A M I I G P A U K A
O Y G N C O N P A L M C T S Y
C T N O W I A L T R P H T I R
R H I L T T F R H E G E E H A
E G L E T U R I T S X N R W M
A I K E O M E A N I N G F U L
T M R M A T U O S G F E L R E
U N A I N S W T P I A A Y R E
R C P S T X E T N O C M C E H
E O S L S N M O D N A R A T Y
C O N K C S P E R R Y N E W S
C T Y E X P A N D E D I O N E
```

Artifacts	Grain	Pine
Awe	Heart	Random
Beach	Infinite	Replica
Butterfly	Magnificent	Sand
Camouflage	Majesty	Sky
Context	Maryann	Snow
Creature	Meaningful	Sparkling
Existence	Mighty	Sperry
Expanded	Owl	Spiritual
Eye	Pattern	Whisked

The Yoga of Gratitude

What are you grateful for? What do you consider the top blessings in your life? Purpose? A sunrise or sunset? An animal companion? A loved one's smile?

Giving thanks and offering gratitude has been with us for a long time. Many offer some form of thanks at meals. *Thank you* has long been taught to children as a magic phrase, along with *please*, the magic word. Prayers of thanks and special ceremonies are common among almost all spiritual traditions. Thanksgiving is a national holiday in several countries. It is sometimes associated more with feasting than with gratitude.

What if we looked at gratitude as a form of yoga? A way to stretch ourselves into a perspective of what is abundant in our lives, not what we lack. Yoga means *union*. When we add a daily practice of stretching our awareness to our many blessings, our lives can and will change and improve. Physical yoga limbers up the body. The yoga of gratitude softens the heart and eases the busy mind.

According to Dr. Paul Mills, professor and director of the Center of Excellence for Research and Training in Integrative Health at the University of California, San Diego, expressing gratitude may actually help us live longer. Counting our blessings counts. His research shows that heart patients who cultivate an attitude of gratitude have less inflammation in their bodies and have better autonomic regulation of their heart. His patients keep a gratitude journal, writing down most days of the week a few things they are grateful for.

Two other recent studies have incorporated procedures intended to foster gratitude into interventions for cancer patients, with favorable results.* Pain patients report that the more they focus on being grateful, the better they are able to manage their pain. Gratitude reduces the heart rate, eases stress, lowers blood pressure, and can help regulate the nervous system. Some patients even say that their thankfulness quotient actually reduces their symptoms.

Sometimes when we think about gratitude, our minds jump to what we don't have enough of. For many that includes time, money, and connection with family/tribe. What about being grateful for basic things that most of us take for granted? Hot and cold running water. Shelter from the storm. A safe place to sleep. Lights that turn on with the flip of a switch. Endless food of incredible variety. Abundant water that is safe to drink. Access to medical care.

It's pretty astounding how rich we are, regardless of the state of our finances. Funny thing about humans; we tend to stress and obsess over what we don't have rather than feel constantly grateful for what we do.

Somewhere in the midst of all that concern about paying this bill or getting to that appointment, consider your blessings. Being alive and functional at whatever level is a big one. Do you have a beloved animal companion? Think for a moment on all that creature has brought to your world. Most of us smile fondly and shake our heads at the same time at adorable, silly, or occasionally destructive antics.

---

*Published on the US Department of Health & Human Services National Institutes of Health National Center for Biotechnology Information website.

Check it out in your own life. Observe and follow your thoughts for a random five minutes. Where does your mind go? Do you worry? Stress? Plan? Organize? Daydream? Are you in the present moment? The past? The future? Interesting to track, isn't it?

Think of the relationships you do have, or did have, that you treasure. Got one very good friend? You're lucky. Remember to celebrate that person and tell them that you do! A special family member that warms your heart and life? Let them know. We think of gratitude as an internal, private thing, and it can be. It can also be shared. Sometimes those that we are most grateful for might not even know it. Surprise them with a special card or long-distance chat. It's good for your health. And it feels wonderful!

What if that special friend or family member has already gone before you into the great beyond? That doesn't have to keep you from celebrating them or remembering the joys and trials you shared. Set aside some time to remember them, talk to them in your thoughts, and feel the love. Visit your special place, have lunch at your shared favorite restaurant, or an indoor picnic of remembrance. Might bring some tears along with the joy, but the joy will be there. Thankfulness can transform.

No matter our health condition, loneliness factor, or state of being, an attitude of gratitude positively impacts our lives. Many enjoy taking some time every day to record at least one thing for which they are thankful. It can be easiest to do this when you get up in the morning and/or right before going to bed. It's constantly available; there's no waiting for open business hours. We can do it in the middle of those unexpected sleepless nights. It's a great cure for insomnia. It can take a week or so to get into the swing of it. It's surprising to discover that the more we look at our lives with gratitude, the more we have to be thankful for.

Changing habits, especially habits of thinking, take time and a bit of effort. Rome wasn't built in a day. If we're habitual worriers, blessing counting can seem strange, false, and even a little bit uncomfortable. Persevere. The benefits are huge and the cost is only a bit of focused attention.

Experiment with what the yoga of gratitude can do for you. Think long and deeply about what is excellent in your life. Watch the stress melt away. Keep blessings uppermost in your mind and heart each and every day.

Enjoy better health and more happiness. Feeling vulnerable, or filled with self-doubt? Practice thankfulness yoga and watch your life fill up and your inner cup of love overflow. Cultivate that attitude of gratitude and see your life transform.

Vulnerability

It's not always easy to be vulnerable. With others, or even simply with ourselves. Asking for help can feel like admitting to a weakness or an incapability. In fact, it takes incredible strength to let someone know we're struggling. Vulnerability is a healthy exercise. Hard times are opportunities to practice the art of opening ourselves to another's compassion and wisdom. We are often surprised at the clarity we can achieve when we add a trusted one's intuition to our own. Talking things over with friends really does help.

Practicing vulnerability does not stop at asking for help. When was the last time you told someone about the little things that make you smile? Have you lately expressed to someone how much they mean to you? It's time to start accessing these valuable pieces of ourselves. Once we are at home with our innermost feelings, sharing them will feel more comfortable.

When we share our feelings and let our inner selves show, we open ourselves to deep connections that enrich our lives. Others will want to share, too. We begin attracting to ourselves more souls that will sing in harmony with us. We find that we are part of a marvelous network of kindred spirits, a community that will care for one another and smile together through life.

—Kaley Elizabeth Oliver

Life Wisdom:

— —— ————————————————
————————— ——————————— ———
————————— ————— —— —————

```
I G M A R V E L O U S E R A C
A M N I C N L A R I T Y O T C
S E N I H H Y T I N U M M O C
T W T I S E I O H Z S P N A S
R I L L L L E Y C A M I P N N
E S V I U B T P V S I B I N I
N D N G O A C Y S E O R E L M
G O P A S R D I H E I T N T E
T M I S S E O Y L T W O S E H
H I O T R N E B S O L H D E A
N A N D I L A D R I A A N M R
C O N N A U M K V R R M E O M
U I N K L V T E E T N I I H O
K E T A Y I R N N T O M R Y N
R L V I F S G N I L E E F E Y
```

Achieve	Harmony	Oliver
Art	Healthy	Share
Care	Help	Sing
Clarity	Home	Smile
Community	Inner	Souls
Compassion	Intuition	Spirits
Elizabeth	Kaley	Strength
Enrich	Kindred	Valuable
Feelings	Marvelous	Vulnerable
Friends	Network	Wisdom

The Healing Power of Laughter

Laughter really is the best medicine.

When I am under stress, one of the things that works for me is to watch a funny movie or TV show that genuinely makes me laugh. YouTube is an endless source of humorous material. My personal favorites include Robin Williams and Don Rickles. I find the comedic genius of these legends very helpful in lifting my mood. The tension in my body and negative thought patterns seem to melt away.

We all go through stressful times in our lives. Jobs are lost. Loved ones die. Divorce happens. We struggle with health issues. It feels inescapable.

Each one of us has developed our own ways of coping with stress. Some people go to the gym for a workout or yoga. I like to do deep breathing and stretching exercises. Others like to get their hands in the dirt through gardening. Some look to water, either swimming or soaking. Others channel their energy in a creative way like dancing, singing, painting, playing music, sculpting, and so on. Many turn to cooking or cleaning or sorting to shift their mood. Some may choose alternatives that may not be so healthful and life-affirming.

My favorite stress coping skill is laughter. When I need to uplift my spirit, I am so glad that I have comedy to turn to. Laughter is so good for the soul! It is nature's healing miracle.

—*Gerlando Compilati*

Life Wisdom:

— —————— —— —— ———

—————— —— ———— ——————

```
A  C  I  S  U  M  L  I  F  T  I  N  G  C
G  G  N  I  P  O  C  A  S  O  U  L  I  A
H  N  S  U  O  R  O  M  U  H  E  D  A  G
R  G  I  T  Y  G  H  C  I  G  E  A  H  O
C  E  M  T  A  A  N  T  H  M  H  N  D  Y
O  R  O  H  P  I  A  I  O  A  I  T  L  A
O  L  O  R  B  L  T  C  K  I  N  T  E  C
K  A  D  O  I  F  U  R  Y  A  H  N  L  R
I  N  R  P  I  G  H  C  I  E  O  E  E  E
N  D  M  L  E  E  S  C  S  D  A  S  L  L
G  O  P  N  A  P  O  P  H  N  E  A  R  C
C  U  I  L  I  M  E  D  I  C  I  N  E  A
L  U  I  R  E  G  E  N  E  R  G  Y  W  R
S  N  I  D  Y  T  G  F  U  N  N  Y  O  I
G  T  Y  M  S  E  L  K  C  I  R  H  P  M
```

Channel	Genius	Music
Cleaning	Gerlando	Power
Comedic	Gym	Rickles
Comedy	Healing	Robin
Compilati	Humorous	Sculpting
Cooking	Laughter	Soaking
Coping	Lifting	Soul
Dirt	Medicine	Spirit
Energy	Miracle	Uplift
Funny	Mood	Yoga

Perspective Changes Everything

Have you ever just wanted to punch a well-meaning person? Those people who say things like: "Everything happens for a reason." "God never gives us more than we can bear." "Why did you create *that* in your life?" "Aren't you over that *yet*?"

People can be insensitive clods. For the grieving, for the suffering, for the caretakers that are barely hanging on by a thread, sometimes the platitudes can feel like the straw that didn't just break the camel's back, but flattened it altogether and turned it into a camel rug. We know they mean well. But....

Here's the other side of the punching bag. Don't hit me!

A while back I decided to experiment with approaching my life from the belief that *every single thing that happens, no matter what it is, is for my highest and best good.* (Another phrase that drives people bonkers.) The Universe, of course, tested me right away. I needed a crown replaced. My chronic health condition comes from dental trauma and infection, so I didn't see any way that this could be for my "highest and best." Except the price. That was definitely highest.

Turns out I had a cavity under the crown, such that I could have lost the tooth. So, much to my surprise, it really was highest and best. And I had a wonderful friend go with me, so I felt supported through the whole episode. First good experience in the dental chair in my life. Amazing.

The stories we tell ourselves matter. Reframing the hard stuff can help us cope and put things in perspective. And keep us from smacking insensitive clods in the face.

—*Melissa Morgan*

Life Wisdom:

— — —   — — — — —   — —   — — — — — — —

— — — — — — — — — —   — — — — — — — —

— — — —   — — — —   — — —

```
T C W P H S U P P O R T E D T E
P L A L O E M O R G A N P W S G
E O R A B R X B O N K E R S E N
O D T T E F P P W O R S E P H I
A S S I L E M O E S I D O D G H
E T D T I S R I P R O C O N I T
V C E U E C U E F S I O I E H Y
P E N D F R C R I T G M S P E R
S G T E C T I P P O A T E I V E
E N A S I E E E S R E V I N U V
G I L V N R E P F I I E R M T E
N Z E D E A E E T E E S S L I F
A A T S E B R P E S W L E M A C
H M D A E R H T X D E T S E T I
C A T H J L U F R E D N O W O Y
```

Amazing	Episode	Platitudes
Belief	Everything	Reframing
Best	Experience	Stories
Bonkers	Experiment	Straw
Camel	Friend	Supported
Changes	Good	Surprise
Clods	Highest	Tested
Cope	Melissa	Thread
Crown	Morgan	Universe
Dental	Perspective	Wonderful

24 The Power to Heal

Doctors are amazing. They can set a bone, or stitch a wound, or save a life. They help set the conditions for our healing, but doctors cannot tell the body how to heal. Only the body knows how to heal itself.

Many of us are used to giving responsibility for our overall health into the hands of the external world. Most of us were raised to do this. When we get sick, we say, "It's up to them to heal me."

Doctors can take care of acute situations and guide us. Our long-term healing is ultimately in our own hands. True healing power lives in the body. Our bodies have a unique, powerfully intricate system of healing.

Our bodies reflect the world we live in. If there is an issue, avoid blame. The body is simply responding to the world it is living in. Love the body. Where possible, change the environment and stimuli it gets. Watch the responses to the changes and adjust as needed.

It is critical that we each recognize our own healing power and take charge of our well-being. The body wants to heal. It has extraordinary powers to heal. It has an almost unlimited pharmacy within to manufacture the compounds it needs. To be committed to the healing, learn to look to the wisdom within and combine it with the information from the health care arena.

Understand that the ability and the power to restore your health lives inside you. Get professional guidance and create a healing environment for the body. Access your inner wisdom. Unleash your healing power.

—*Elizabeth Kipp*

Life Wisdom:

— — — — — — —   — — — —   — — —   — — —

— — — —   — — —   — — — — — — —   — — — — — —

```
N R H E A L I N G L E A R N E
H O A C C E S S C C C P P I K
T M I B O D Y A O O E V O L T
E E O T D E T I M I L N U S G
B T D N A I Z P B A E T U Y R
A S H O A M O T I Y Z J T E O
Z Y U A C U R R N R D I N E E
I S Y O N T U O E A L N N T G
L R O D W N O S F I I T A G U
E G S R E A T R B N T C H H I
U W I S D O M A S E I E C E D
Q P H A R M A C Y R V L T A A
I S R E W O P T T A H F I L N
N N I H T I W N S E A E T T C
U L I L U M I T S E R R S H E
```

Ability	Healing	Reflect
Access	Health	Restore
Adjust	Information	Save
Amazing	Inner	Stimuli
Body	Intricate	Stitch
Combine	Kipp	System
Compounds	Learn	Unique
Doctors	Love	Unlimited
Elizabeth	Pharmacy	Wisdom
Guidance	Power	Within

Listen for Your Inner Wisdom

Most of us have heard voices inside our heads. Discerning where they're coming from is important. So is our mental health. The chatter can sometimes make us feel crazy. Other times, we've heard profoundly intuitive advice that changed the course of our lives for the better.

Meditation, mindfulness, and professional guidance can help us make sense of the chatter. To be able to connect with the helpful, knowing voices for advice, like consulting with our own personal wisdom council, we need to take time in silence to listen carefully.

To begin, find a quiet space to sit. Have a pen and paper ready. Wisdom's truths are so profound and affirming you won't want to miss a single word. Relax. Breathe deeply and ask, "Wisdom, are you here?" Wait until you hear, "Yes." Now ask, "What information can you share with me today?" Listen for the words and write them down. Write exactly what you hear. Be open. Allow the words to flow through you onto the page.

Be patient. The process will become easier each time. The conversations we record and the explorations we uncover are well worth the time. The messages of inner Wisdom can astonish, transform, and renew us. Keep them in a safe place as they are a wealth of trusted information to refer to often.

Throughout our lives, our loving guides have been watching over us. They are always with us to encourage and inspire. Our inner Wisdom is an endless haven, a refuge, and a guiding light for the ever-changing outer world in which we dwell. All we have to do is listen carefully.

—*Debbie Clark*

Life Wisdom:

__ __ __   __ __ __ __   __ __ __ __ __ __   __ __   __

__ __ __ __ __ __   __ __   __ __ __ __   __ __ __ __ __ __ __

__ __ __   __ __ __ __ __   __ __ __ __ __

```
E V I T I U T N I N R E Y O E
S E C I O V U R M I E E G C N
L E R E N E W R N E R T N A W
I G W I S D O M I I S E S N P
C U D O E F M I S N L A S I I
N F O U S N R C E I S O F A L
U E D N L E C A S E P P F K N
O R A L L H G O D O W F I P I
C R E I A D U N U V I G A R W
T W G V E L I N W R I D G O E
D H E B O A D R M R A C E F A
T N B V L C I I A T T G E O L
R I I L P T N E I T A P E U T
E N O E E G G U C L A R K N H
G W N U T A S T O N I S H D H
```

Advice	Haven	Profound
Affirming	Inner	Refuge
Allow	Inspire	Renew
Astonish	Intuitive	Silence
Clark	Light	Transform
Council	Listen	Uncover
Debbie	Loving	Voices
Dwell	Page	Wealth
Encourage	Patient	Wisdom
Guiding	Pen	Write

It's a Process

The phrase *it's a process* is how I think about my long-term goals and plans. It helps me work around those unexpected incidents that occur.

A perfectly planned day can be challenging to execute. Things like rain, or a surprise visitor, or a traffic jam just happen; happy about it or not! When we trust the process, it feels like a river flowing. This flow helps us with the Big Kahunas in life. You know, those occurrences that are a ten on the one-to-ten scale of life importance.

Health. Definitely a process. Well-being is physical, mental, spiritual, and social wholeness and arguably the most precious spectrum we attend to in life. A sudden health event, one's own or a loved one's, can upset our equilibrium. It is when we regain composure and focus on navigating the next steps that the process of healing flows.

Forgiveness. We don't plan to forgive. We also don't plan to be betrayed. When there is a tear in the fabric of our being, devotion to and trust in the incremental process of forgiveness restores wholeness.

Grief. Loss is one of the most jarring twists along life's path. When we acknowledge endings, including all the *little deaths*, like trading in a beloved car or giving up a habit, we embrace the natural ebb and flow of life.

Commitment. When I've felt most elated about making a commitment, like having a child or opening my business, I also felt like there was shifting sand under my feet. It would have been much scarier if I had not trusted my Guidance, myself, and the process of learning every day along the way.

—*Denise Lewis Premschak*

Life Wisdom:

_ _ _ _ _   _ _ _   _ _ _ _ _ _ _   _ _

_ _ _ _   _ _   _ _ _ _ _ _   _ _

_ _ _ _ _ _   _ _ _   _ _   _ _ _ _ _   _ _

_ _ _ _ _   _ _ _ _ _ _ _ _

```
T N R U B M E N T A L E W I S
S O T T G U W H O L E N E S S
P I H E F R S L A C I S Y H P
R T P R O T I I O C E S E R I
O O S O C C F E N L I A E T R
C V F E U E T O F E L M W R I
E E U N S P F O L T S I O U T
S D R I D S A S H C S S L S U
S A N U H A K P H T L U F T A
C E D S S A N A S N E O D A L
D N D L L O K F O R G I V E I
N N W A I A P Y S S O C I A L
A W E N E H O M V E R E B I G
S I M A G I C G O C I R B A F
T N E M T I M M O C N P E E D
```

Big	Flow	Precious
Business	Focus	Premschak
Car	Forgive	Process
Child	Goals	Sand
Commitment	Grief	Social
Composure	Health	Spectrum
Denise	Kahunas	Spiritual
Devotion	Lewis	Trust
Ebb	Mental	Twists
Fabric	Physical	Wholeness

Accepting What Is

When we expand beyond life's challenges, and have more peace in our lives, it is a good thing. One way to do that is to consider just accepting *what is*. Yep, no matter *what* it is, or how it feels! What does it mean to accept what is? It means that we release any fear, doubt, or worry about a situation, person, or outcome. It's our choice to decide that we will no longer stress ourselves about things that are out of our control. We will focus, instead, on what we *can* control: ourselves.

I use the mantra, "I don't mind what happens." It's one of my favorite mental exercises. I admit it's not always easy and, yet, it is amazing what it can do when things in life are not going the way I had hoped.

When I tell people of my "I don't mind what happens" practice, I hear gasps of, "Oh, no, I can't do that, I care too much." I have to reply that it doesn't mean that you don't care. Absolutely we care. Not *minding* doesn't change that. Powerful things happen within when we *don't mind what happens*. First, the way we see things changes and then our whole being just relaxes into what is, with no resistance.

When we release resistance, we provide ourselves an opportunity to see through what we think *should* be and see how something *could* be. This powerful practice allows us to engage with life, not fight with it. We can look to the possibility of resolving the issues or simply relax into what is happening, not minding, and allow it all to flow.

—*Darity Wesley*

Life Wisdom:

— —————— —— —— —— —————

—— —— ———— ——— ——— —————

————— —————————

```
C S E S I C R E X E I C H O O
S A O E T R O E S A B E R L W
A C R P M T E C M P L E P U O
E H D E P E H L T O S E E F L
N A S N M O N A E I C A R R L
G L C N I A R T S A M T G E A
A L W C E M N T A P S D U W N
G E E E I P A T U L E E A O Y
E N S N M N P L R N Y A I P T
F G L L C E O A I A I T C F I
L E E E C R E A H S A T N E R
O S Y C T D N O U U T M Y I A
W N A N P R A C T I C E D W D
H A O E T H O I A N O S R E P
P C Y P E F S N S D N A P X E
```

Accept	Expand	Peace
Admit	Flow	Person
Allow	Focus	Powerful
Care	Gasps	Practice
Challenges	Happens	Relax
Choice	Mantra	Release
Control	Mental	Resistance
Darity	Mind	Situation
Engage	Opportunity	Wesley
Exercises	Outcome	Yep

28 **Happily Ever Now**

To become whole as human beings, we can decide to manifest heaven on Earth and not have to wait for happily ever after. We can create *happily ever now.*

As one of seven children, I was raised in a chaotic, Christian home. Both of my parents had serious, multiple addictions. To remember my childhood (much of which was missing; forgotten due to trauma), I began making paintings using my own family photos and home movies as source material. As I walked this path, I became passionate to know how the distilled wisdom of world religions is taught in the homes of families practicing other faiths.

I reached these conclusions: It is my belief that the people on Earth live within webs of cultural and social forces, much as stars and planets exist within webs of natural forces that both bind them together and keep them apart. Though we seem to live as separate individuals, nations, cultures, and faiths—in truth, we are one in our humanity.

Earth is our home. Humans are family.

I believe that every person can awaken to their own inner teacher. I found the truth about my own life. To do this, I have had to trudge the road to my happy destiny. Because my childhood was so difficult, this trudge has not been easy or fun; however, my experience has proven to me that it beats the alternative of staying numb to my feelings, dissociating, and feeling separated from love within me.

With a focus on finding love that is true love, I believe each of us can create our own happiness. Each of us can live happily ever now.

—*Heidi Hardin*

Life Wisdom:

— — — — — — — — — — — — — — — — — — —

— — — — — — — — — — — — — — — — —

```
S F N Y S S M A N I F E S T
N I O O P R E N E V E R H H
A D L R W P A R L O V E A A
M I W I C T A T U V H S R P
U E E H I E L H S T S I D P
H H M O O A S E R E L N I I
T P N O I L G A N H E U N L
S S A C V D E I S B E W C Y
T M O I U I P Y N I T S E D
E S O R N P E M S E N I T F
N A T N A T D S E H N N A J
A O Y H L I I F E N T M A S
L H E A V E N N E I I I T C
P N E K A W A R G L O M A E
R E H C A E T S Y S O N E F
```

Awaken	Happy	Now
Cultures	Hardin	One
Destiny	Heaven	Paintings
Earth	Heidi	Planets
Ever	Humans	Social
Faiths	Inner	Stars
Family	Love	Teacher
Forces	Manifest	Trudge
Happily	Movies	Webs
Happiness	Nations	Whole

29   Just Enough Birthdays

Lately, I find myself checking the birth dates of hospice patients I visit. I wonder if the patient is too young to die. Most people would rather die when they get *old*. But when does *old* happen? 65? 75? 90?

I meet folks in their nineties who imply they are too young to go because they still have things to do. A few patients in their eighties may question why they've lived so long and want God to "get on with it already."

As a chaplain, I've attended a lot of deaths of people too young to die—infants, children, young mothers, and soldiers. Seeing those early deaths, I can only guess what my reaction would be if I contracted a terminal illness now. Would I consider myself of qualified age and be grateful for the years I've had? Would it be selfish or ungrateful of me to pray for more time?

This musing gives rise to the scripture from Hebrews 9:27, "It is appointed unto a man, once to die and after this the judgement." The judgement I want us to consider is self-judgement—now, in the present tense.

With that in mind, here's my prayer asking God for just enough birthdays and just enough chances:

Help me seek forgiveness from those I've wronged.
Guide me to grant forgiveness to those who need your healing touch.
Help me sow seeds of love in those who feel unloved.
Show me how to infuse joy in those who are joyless.
Give me understanding to share with those who thirst for it.
Most of all, help me be authentic in my witness for You.

—*Chaplain Norris Burkes*

Life Wisdom:

__ ____ _ ____ ____ __ ___

_____ __ _ _____ ___

_ ___

```
A  L  G  I  F  E  E  Y  A  D  H  T  R  I  B
W  E  C  R  S  I  R  R  O  N  F  L  S  T  C
L  L  H  N  A  Y  O  J  U  O  I  S  L  O  H
J  V  I  B  O  T  E  D  R  T  E  O  O  U  A
F  U  L  A  U  W  E  G  N  N  P  Y  V  C  N
L  S  D  D  E  R  I  F  T  I  P  I  E  H  C
S  N  R  G  E  V  K  I  U  A  R  G  R  I  E
T  T  E  E  E  A  W  E  T  L  A  G  T  C  S
S  H  N  N  H  M  T  I  S  P  Y  N  G  T  S
I  W  E  A  S  T  E  H  A  A  E  I  N  N  B
L  S  E  E  F  N  O  N  S  H  R  S  I  E  S
S  S  I  R  T  N  N  M  T  C  G  U  L  S  A
N  D  A  S  B  J  I  U  G  O  D  M  A  E  O
G  N  U  O  Y  E  A  S  O  L  D  I  E  R  S
E  C  I  P  S  O  H  E  N  O  U  G  H  P  Y
```

Authentic	Grateful	Norris
Birthday	Healing	Now
Burkes	Hebrews	Patients
Chances	Hospice	Prayer
Chaplain	Infants	Present
Children	Joy	Scripture
Deaths	Judgement	Soldiers
Enough	Love	Touch
Forgiveness	Mothers	Witness
God	Musing	Young

30   ## 94 Years Wise

I just celebrated my ninety-fourth birthday. Reflecting on the learning of my life, here's my advice:

Be kind to others. Kindness matters. It's how we all like to be treated. A great kindness is to smile and look at people as they pass by on the street. I remember a time when I was at my daughter's home and feeling quite ill. A young girl walking by looked right at me and smiled beautifully and sincerely. That heartwarming feeling still remains.

Listen and help those in need. Listening is a gift. Often it is a great help to have a trusted person with whom to share trying circumstances or deep thoughts.

No regrets or living in the past. One can never go back and live differently than one has. Every decision along life's way is made using one's experiences up until that time.

With God's help, forgive ourselves for all we have failed. It feels a little like repenting when I review my day at bedtime and ask forgiveness so I can release the burden of those things I would like to have done better or differently.

Always tell the truth. Even when another doesn't want to hear it, it is better for one's own heart.

Bless and love your family, each and every one, and always show them your best self. Be an example of harmony. This will be returned to you again and again.

—Betty Lewis

Life Wisdom:

— — — —, — — — — — — —, — — — — — — — —,

— — — — — — — — — — —, — — —

— — — — — — — — — — — — — — — — — —

— — — — — — — — — — — — —

```
E R A H S S L O Y R E V I E W
N E D R U B I A T R U S T E D
H E V Y E H D N A R I R V M M
Y T L O L H N Y C W A I K I I
T L U I T I N D E E G N E T S
S F L R M F M L H R R O O D C
R G I U T S I A O V E E D E N
H B E G F T S F F S A B L B N
A A D N O I S I C E D E E Y L
R D I S T L T E E N B T H I N
M V G H I B E U B R T T E E L
O I P S L K R V A Y S E L M O
N C T E I O G T O E T R P H T
Y E S N H E E P A L B T H I N
N S D L I D R E L E A S E F E
```

Advice	Decision	Listen
Beautifully	Family	Love
Bedtime	Forgive	Regrets
Best	Gift	Release
Better	God	Review
Betty	Harmony	Share
Birthday	Heart	Sincerely
Bless	Help	Smile
Burden	Kind	Trusted
Celebrated	Lewis	Truth

The Cycles of Life

Where are you in the cycles of life? The success years? The young professional? Starting a family? Legacy time?

We celebrate our birthdays as an annual cycle of life. We drink champagne or other sparkler to acknowledge the New Year. There are the cycles of the moon. There are seven-year cycles, astrological cycles, fashion cycles, business, financial, and news cycles. Bicycles, tricycles, and unicycles. Our biological clocks are ticking.

Which came first, the chicken or the egg?

We are part of life on the planet, not separate from it. We are conceived, born, grow, mature, age, die, and then whatever happens after. Nobody gets out of here alive. No one lives without loss. All Earth inhabitants experience the same cycles: seed, sprout, growth, blossom, fruit, wither, die, and compost. All matter is a matter of life and death.

Every seven-to-ten years we become essentially new people, because in that time, every cell in our bodies has been replaced by a new cell. Don't you feel younger than you were ten years ago? Refreshed, renewed, and reinvigorated?

Each cell has an individual life span. When they die off, they are replaced with new cells. From one perspective, our body is an Earth suit of fifty-to-seventy-five trillion cells, living, dying, and being renewed every single moment. Mind boggling, isn't it? How deep down the rabbit hole do you want to go?

When a human expires their last breath, it may take hours or days before all the cells in the body die. That's how forensic investigators can determine the time of death. Red blood cells live for about four months. White blood cells live more or less for a week. Skin cells live a couple of weeks. Our brain cells typically last an entire lifetime. We create new ones even into our elder years. We can retrain our brain cells through the power of neuroplasticity. That's part of why we do puzzles. To stay fresh and keep our brains growing.

We get to practice the cycles of life every single day. We wake up, reborn, from our night's sleep. We experience the day and, at the end, relinquish our bodies back to sleep. Perchance to dream? What is the space beyond the body, the dreamtime, the void?

What happens after we die?

Most religious traditions believe that what we humans do in life echoes in eternity. They teach that eternal life is of the soul, not the body. Some religions, including Christianity, Islam, and Judaism, believe in the soul's existence in another afterlife. Other religions, like many forms of Hinduism and Buddhism, believe in reincarnation. Still others yet, like the spectrum of Pagan belief systems, can include a combination or even a blending of afterlife and reincarnation. Whatever the specificity of their beliefs, Americans are strongly spiritual. 92 percent believe in God, and 74 percent believe in life after death.*

No one knows the answers to these questions. There is no scientific proof one way or another. There is quite a controversy around the issue. Like all human belief systems, including religion, some say *yay*, some say *nay*, and some say *I don't know.*

There is a special time in the cycle of life, death, and rebirth in nature when we pull up last season's dying plants and compost them. During this time of the void, the land lies fallow, and nothing much appears to happen. Yet beneath the surface, the earth is preparing itself for new life to come.

---

*2015 Pew Forum on Religion and Public Life

In human life, in the Tibetan Buddhist tradition, that in-between time is called the *bardo*. Bardos actually occur continuously in our lives. They are junctures of possibility and what quantum physics calls "potential." It's the white space between activities, where we integrate and recharge. It's that week of holiday between Christmas and New Year's, of time away from our normal schedules. When we sleep, it is the dreamtime between nodding off and waking up. Pure *be* time rather than *do* time.

Most of us are not trained to recognize, much less maximize, these times. We are encouraged by society to avoid our empty spaces or fill them up quickly with distractions. We are led to believe it is easier to endure the pain of the known, rather than face the overwhelming potential of the unknown. The void, like the womb, is a fertile space in which new realities are created.

When you find yourself at the powerful threshold of a bardo, cherish it as sacred personal time. Consider some ideas and intentions for this rich and creative moment. Be willing to sit, for a time, with the emptiness, and discover what it may bring. Re-dream and reinvent yourself. Gestate your world so when the cycle shifts, you will be able to birth the new you that you intend.

By using the natural cycles for our personal growth, we engage the support of the world around us in our quest for a higher quality, more meaningful life. Embrace transitions. Life cycles always include change. Death is not the enemy. We are all at the beginning, and at the end, every day.

Stand for Yourself

My parents and most of my aunts and uncles were sharecroppers, all born in Arkansas during the early 1900s. We fled in 1937—with a lynch mob preparing to hang my uncle for trying to unionize sharecroppers. I was three. Ultimately, we landed in San Diego, California.

As an adult, I was a five-foot two-inch black woman knocking on doors, in largely white working-class neighborhoods, to either collect past due monies, or physically turn off the gas and electric valves. I was called every name imaginable. Enduring verbal abuses came with the job. I had a family to feed. I had no other option but to thicken my skin, and call in the police when threats escalated.

As an eighty-six-year-old black woman who's lived through and experienced pretty much every possible gender and racial inequality that exists, melded with sprinkles of domestic violence, here are my words of wisdom:

- Stand up for what you believe in. Be heard. Make your presence felt.
- Stay focused on your purpose and goals. Don't allow the small stuff to take you off track.
- Don't tolerate abuse. Once you're free, trust there's a better life waiting for you.
- A closed mouth doesn't get fed. Ask for what you deserve. Challenge unfair treatment.

—*Lula Washington*

Life Wisdom:

— —   — — —   — — — —   — — — —   — — — — —

— —   — — — —   — — —   — — —   — — —   — — —

— — — — —   — — —   — — — — — — — —

```
D N T O E C N E S E R P A Y S
E H R O N V T E F T F L L L E
S E A L S A E E H R U I A W E
E A C W R I L I E L M O A T S
R R K E T T C E L A G S S S D
V D L N R K E K F E H L A U R
E O I L E S T G S I B A S R O
T K N N A K D U N A P F N T W
S E O R T Y N G S E V L A V O
U S T H M E T O B M L W K A Y
Y O O U E O S T C E O L R A N
S P R I N K L E S K T D A D F
O R R Y T S T A N D I T S H O
U U R M O U T H F E D N E I C
S P F O C U S E D E L F G R W
```

Arkansas	Free	Stand
Ask	Goals	Thicken
Believe	Heard	Tolerate
Better	Knocking	Track
Challenge	Lula	Treatment
Deserve	Mouth	Trust
Family	Presence	Valves
Fed	Purpose	Washington
Felt	Skin	Wisdom
Focused	Sprinkles	Words

Resilience

The ability to bounce back when adversity hits is what resilience is about. We all are innately strong and durable. Sometimes we just need to be reminded of it and have concrete ways to strengthen it.

There are several techniques that can help raise our resilience factor. Some of these include flexibility in our thinking, overload management, determination, gumption, emotional first aid, and firming up support.

There are four essential pillars to building resilience. First, recognize and understand that change is actually possible. The next two pillars guide us to think and also accurately assess both strengths and weaknesses. And finally, take the time to focus on those strengths and draw upon them to sustain and fortify ourselves.

To build resilience, we must pause and ask, how do you feel? Is your stress level in the danger zone? Do you feel overwhelmed and in a fight-or-flight mentality? If that is the case, it is time to address your resilience level.

First, recognize the adversity. Ask yourself, what is the belief that I have taken from this issue? Then begin to think, what do I hope for here? What is a likely outcome? What else could happen? What strategies and strengths can I draw upon?

Slow down and take into account what the underlying belief is. We can evaluate the next step that we want to take. We are in a resilient state of mind. We have the flexibility, knowledge of our own strengths, and resolve to move ahead.

—*Kamini Wood*

Life Wisdom:

___ ___ ___ ___ ___   ___ ___ ___ ___ ___

___ ___ ___ ___   ___ ___   ___ ___   ___ ___ ___ ___

___ ___ ___   ___ ___ ___   ___ ___ ___ ___   ___ ___ ___ ___ ___

___ ___   ___ ___ ___

```
B E Y T I L I B A C C O U N T C
F E I L E B S C O R E S O L V E
S C M M I N O T G Y F I T R O F
U N E O R N E S R I T D O O W T
C U C L C P I L L A R S I E R N
O O N R S T R E N G T H S O T A
F B E L L K U I O P W E P S A U
N T I S A S M O S A T P G O D E
E O L M S R O S U U U V E I V R
C O I E E L B I S S O P S A E M
E N S T V P A I T E N T L A R S
I S E N P E D O A T R U H E S R
A D R O B M L S I O A D T A I C
L E L B A R U D N T E S D I T N
L I F C H A N G E D I U G A Y E
```

Ability	Durable	Pillars
Account	Evaluate	Possible
Address	Focus	Resilience
Adversity	Fortify	Resolve
Assess	Guide	Strategies
Belief	Gumption	Strengths
Bounce	Kamini	Strong
Change	Level	Support
Concrete	Outcome	Sustain
Determination	Pause	Wood

33 The Opportunity of Challenge

Life is full of contrasts.

There are wonderful days when we are on top of everything. We succeed and accomplish all we want. Our dreams seem close. Don't you really love days like that? And appreciate the results!

Then there are more difficult days when life seems to be flying by out of control. Those days are frustrating but they have a great deal of value. Perhaps it's time to pause and reconsider how to pursue our goals.

In either type of energy, it is important to stay focused upon the desired outcome. Focus will manifest a result. The result may be a major success or a bigger challenge. Either of these is an opportunity. This perspective has helped me through some pretty difficult circumstances in my life and has shown me how to navigate through them, learning as I go.

Who would focus on challenges? Nobody wants challenges! But if that were true, we wouldn't know how to walk or talk or do any of the things that we take for granted now.

It would be ridiculous to say, "There is nothing I can't do," and equally foolish to say, "I am afraid to try something too difficult." Move through life step-by-step. Observe the results you are creating. Refine your technique as you go. This is the way to view life as a learning opportunity.

Remember, the bigger the challenge, the more rewarding the accomplishment.

—Ingrid Coffin

Life Wisdom:

___ ___ ___ ___ ___ ___ ___ ___

___ ___ ___ ___ ___ ___ ___ ___

___ ___ ___ ___ ___ ___

```
L I B I G G E R V I E W L P F
E C H A L L E N G E N I U O S
F O S R Y F L E T E A G F T R
N I N U I T U A K L A W R N R
G A N N C S I E S U A P E I D
N L E O R C G N I Y L F D F D
A O U U E R E C U H A I N F L
V V P R W G Y E L T C E O O N
I E P D A G N T D U R G W C E
G P S R R H S I L P M O C C A
A A R E D E P O N U S K P O W
T E N A I R U F U R S U L P L
E E T M N S T E P E A E C A O
A C H S G O B S E R V E R O T
E R V A L U E G O A L S L S F
```

Accomplish	Ingrid	Rewarding
Appreciate	Learning	Ridiculous
Bigger	Love	Step
Challenge	Navigate	Succeed
Coffin	Observe	Talk
Dreams	Opportunity	Top
Energy	Pause	Value
Flying	Pursue	View
Focus	Refine	Walk
Goals	Result	Wonderful

34   The Ebb and Flow of Life

The joyous moments of life sustain us. During hard times, it can be difficult to feel and remember the joy. Sometimes we just feel numb.

The challenge is that when we put up barriers against pain, we also put up barriers against joy. To be free, we need to let it all in. Let the emotions flow. The good, the bad, the indifferent. We need to dance to the music of our lives.

Impermanence is the reality we must all grapple with. We will lose many things over the course of our lives. Friends come and go. Loved ones pass away. Buildings eventually crumble. Just because something is temporary does not mean we have to despair. Snow melts and waters the flowers of spring.

Flowers wilt, but give way to seeds and fruits. Cookies and desserts are meant to be consumed. If we only try to have our cake and never eat it, it will eventually go stale. So will we.

It's hard to say goodbye. Even knowing things are temporary, even knowing that everything changes, it doesn't make it hurt any less. We want to be able to hold onto things. We want to be able to love and not let go. Yet holding too tightly onto things is certain to make them break. Sometimes grief is inevitable. Life loses its savor when we focus on fear and pain.

Even in the midst of fear and pain, it is possible to focus on joy. Loss creates depth and teaches us compassion. The sunset is still beautiful. Feeling everything we feel and experience allows us to flow with life. And celebrate when the joy returns.

—*Krista Strom*

Life Wisdom:

__ ___ ____ _____ _____ ___ _____

_____ ___ _____ _____

___ _____ _____ _____

```
T  R  E  F  I  L  D  H  E  K  L  F  E  B
S  E  I  K  O  O  C  E  B  R  O  E  A  N
E  M  T  D  N  F  L  O  S  I  V  E  W  O
B  E  J  A  F  I  L  I  L  S  E  L  F  F
B  M  O  N  E  G  A  U  E  T  E  R  R  E
M  B  Y  I  O  N  F  T  N  A  U  R  E  D
C  E  M  O  T  I  O  N  S  I  S  S  T  S
U  R  S  T  T  R  S  H  T  U  G  D  A  S
A  T  U  U  N  P  O  S  C  R  S  E  R  T
H  I  A  M  D  S  N  O  A  G  I  E  B  T
S  E  E  V  B  E  F  P  E  P  E  S  E  W
B  E  E  R  F  L  P  R  E  C  M  S  L  O
T  W  O  N  S  L  E  T  R  K  N  O  E  L
U  S  D  N  E  I  R  F  H  U  A  A  C  F
L  Y  M  O  R  T  S  G  S  O  N  C  D  E
```

Beautiful	Ebb	Krista
Cake	Emotions	Life
Celebrate	Feel	Love
Compassion	Flow	Remember
Cookies	Focus	Seeds
Crumble	Free	Snow
Dance	Friends	Spring
Depth	Fruits	Strom
Desserts	Grapple	Sunset
Eat	Joy	Sustain

Ask Your Heart

Is the glass half empty, or half full? Could it be both? What if there's room for both perceptions? Or even more choices? How does *how* we look at that glass impact our lives?

Sometimes our hearts are burdened with deep-rooted sadness, regrets, lack of forgiveness, or hatred. These negative thoughts and emotions are a roadblock to our ability to change. They force us to see the glass as half empty and ourselves as less than. When we want to effectively change ourselves to improve our lives, we need to bypass the mind. We need to learn how to listen with our hearts.

Scientists have known since the late 1800s that the heart sends more signals to the brain than vice versa. These signals have profound effects and connections to both the primitive and sophisticated areas of the brain responsible for emotions, perceptions, attention, memory, and problem solving. Not only does the heart respond to the brain, but the brain continuously responds to the heart. The heart is an amazing information-processing and sensory system. It's like a living computer. The circuitry of the heart computer enables that precious, life-giving organ to learn, remember, and make decisions independent of the brain.

The brain has an amazing ability to learn and change. It's called neuroplasticity. So does the heart. Consider a change of heart towards yourself and others. Let go of unkind perceptions and thoughts. Embrace resiliency. Return power to where it belongs, with you. Then you can see that glass however you want. Cheers!

—*Therapy Twins Jane Buckley and Joan Landino*

Life Wisdom:

‗‗‗‗ ‗‗‗ ‗‗ ‗‗‗‗ ‗‗‗‗

‗‗‗‗ ‗‗‗‗‗ ‗‗‗ ‗‗‗‗‗

‗‗‗‗ ‗‗‗‗

```
T Y P A R E H T S L E P L E
L R C A R R N R H O O I C M
W L A N T O E S T W S I O P
H I U E E E N M E T R S M T
N K W F H I G R E C I Y P Y
T H S C W Y L N U M O S U I
U R N T H E A I A R B T T M
T H O U G H T S S H Y E E P
Y Y I T A R N O B E C M R A
S R T D Y C N R L E R E H C
S O O A N I A K G C C E Y T
A M M S D I C A B I L I T Y
L E E N N U O U O O J O A N
G M A R B E M U I H H A L F
S L A N G I S N D C J A N E
```

Ability	Full	Power
Brain	Glass	Precious
Buckley	Half	Remember
Change	Heart	Resiliency
Cheers	Impact	Sensory
Choice	Jane	Signals
Circuitry	Joan	System
Computer	Landino	Therapy
Emotions	Listen	Thoughts
Empty	Memory	Twins

36 Right with Ourselves

Are you okay? What does that even mean? Think about it for a second, or longer. Inside, each of us knows the answer to that question. Some days we are; some days we're not. It can change in a moment.

It's okay to not be okay. We all feel upset sometimes, and that is completely normal. We are not perfect. Our flaws are what make us stand out. We don't have to just *get over it*.

Nobody is okay all the time. Many of us have been told that we'll be okay eventually, and we will! It is okay to want to be okay. It's okay to not want to do or be anything in a moment of despair. Sometimes all that we want to do is feel our emotions and just be. Free to sob our eyes out, scream into the void, or tell people how what they're doing makes us feel. Or laugh aloud with giddy delight.

At times, people like to tell others what to do and how to feel. Just because they tell you, it doesn't mean that they control you. We each have our own emotions. They are ours and ours alone. We don't have to feel a certain way about anything or anyone. Our opinions are ours. Not everyone has to agree on every little thing.

We are not always going to be okay. We do not have to be okay. Knowing that we are all loved by someone, even if that someone is ourselves, means even when life is not okay, we are always truly okay, deep down inside, where it counts.

—*Sophia Cassity*

Life Wisdom:

__ __ __ __ __ __ __ __   __ __ __ __   __ __ __ __ __

__ __ __ __   __ __ __ __   __ __ __ __ __ __ __   __ __ __ __

__ __ __ __ __   __ __ __ __   __ __ __ __ __   __ __   __ __ __

```
C H G U A L Y D E L E R Y T
E G N A H C E T L B R E D H
E F S A T L D O I D E W D G
Y R O Y I O V O U S E S I I
E E P G W E I O T E S N G R
S E H N D N L N R U R A S P
I T I E S A U G O N N N C E
E R A I M O A S E R O L F E
A N D D C O E X P I M L O D
T E F E E L T R N V S A E D
Y N D E S P A I R W O O L N
H A E A T B P E O I N I B O
G O K M K O A Y M N E A D C
N S T O O T E S P U S O Y E
S C R E A M O U S W A L F S
```

Agree	Emotions	Normal
Aloud	Eyes	Okay
Answer	Feel	Opinions
Cassity	Flaws	Right
Change	Free	Scream
Counts	Giddy	Second
Deep	Inside	Sob
Delight	Laugh	Sophia
Despair	Loved	Upset
Down	Moment	Void

The Wisdom of Self-Acceptance

Many of us learned early on that we had to hide parts of ourselves in order to be accepted, or acceptable. These messages may have come from parents, teachers, the media, or even other children. We may have been told off or even punished for showing a side of ourselves that others have a hard time seeing or hearing, let alone accepting.

From an early age, many have been taught that the priority was other people's opinions, rather than accepting the wisdom of our own true thoughts, feelings, and emotions. We learned to hide the precious parts of ourselves that may not be understood by others.

If we grow up believing that it's not safe to show who we are, we hesitate to cry or admit we are scared, weak, or vulnerable. Both boys and girls receive this message.

We need to learn to accept and approve of ourselves, irrespective of what anybody else thinks. We really have nothing to hide. Lying on our deathbeds, are we still going to be wondering, or worrying about, what others think?

We can choose what we think. We can be authentic. We can approve of ourselves no matter what, with all of our flaws. When we do this, we can truly begin to be free.

—Zhana

Life Wisdom:

— — — — — — — — — — — — — — —

— — — — — — — — — — — — — — — — — —

— — — — — — — — —

```
D E R A C S A S A C C S A M E
E O E P E K T U T Y G N A O T
S O P D N H U R T N A I K D A
O S I I G S E L I H D A U S T
O H H U N F U L Z E E N A I I
H T O E N I E O M W D N D W S
C H C L L E O E I E E A T A E
T E R A F B R N R C N T P I H
H M Y D E E A S S F E P P P C
G O A M O F T R Y E R R W A E
I T C I R O A O E O U F P R F
R I C T O Y O S V N B R U E L
L O E D R O W E N S L P T N A
S N P S R E H C A E T U I T W
R S T I M E S S A G E T V S S
```

Accept	Free	Scared
Admit	Girls	Teachers
Approve	Hesitate	Think
Authentic	Hide	Thoughts
Boys	Media	True
Choose	Message	Understood
Cry	Opinions	Vulnerable
Emotions	Parents	Weak
Feelings	Precious	Wisdom
Flaws	Safe	Zhana

It's a Wonderful Life

Although I am young, with much to learn and experience, I know how I want to live. Here's my plan to create a wonderful life. First, find your people. Find like-minded people who have similar dreams. Being selective about who you let into your inner circle is important for the real world.

Let's face it, we're not going to be friends with every person we meet. That doesn't mean we have to be impolite to them. William Shakespeare wrote, "Love all, trust a few, do wrong to none." This is a good philosophy. I would revise it. Respect all, trust a few, do wrong to none.

Second, we all need to go out of our way to question things in life. Not everything is as it seems. There are many viewpoints to consider when it comes to religion, politics, and philosophy. When growing up, children can benefit from questioning the environment around them rather than immediately accepting what authority figures tell them. This way they can learn to create their own identity with their own unique thoughts.

Third, don't compromise what you believe in and are passionate about. Not for anyone. No one knows you better than you do. Letting others tell us what to do, especially if it goes against our own grain, is a recipe for disaster. Although the outside world can influence our paths, we are each primarily responsible for our own lives and choices.

—*Susannah Spalding*

Life Wisdom:

— — — —   — — — —   — — — — — — —,   — — —
— — — — — — — — —,   — — —   — —
— — — — — — — —   — — — — — — — — — — —

```
T W R O N G F C S E T A E R C
S B E L I E V E H R I N L E N
U Y O U N G L D E O Y O U V A
R U R P S E E V O P I L F O L
T E A F C U I S K Q T C R L P
U E E T E S S Y T I T N E D I
S W I H E S T A F I O T D S N
R V R O S M I E N C A A N E N
E I E U D A N M E N I B O F E
S N C G Y E O E O U A R W I U
P N I H B R R I L R Q H C L S
E E P T E D S L E P P I A L F
C R E S U S N A S N O M N L E
T H S P A L D I N G O E O U L
A M E P D P A T H S L N P C Y
```

All	Inner	Revise
Believe	Life	Selective
Benefit	Love	Spalding
Choices	None	Susannah
Circle	Passionate	Thoughts
Compromise	Paths	Trust
Create	People	Unique
Dreams	Plan	Wonderful
Few	Recipe	Wrong
Identity	Respect	Young

39 The Power of Imagination

Our minds are like supercomputers. We get to decide what we put in the search function. We may not fully understand the algorithms, but they work on our behalf.

Take inventory of your life. Have gratitude for your blessings. Notice the items on your lists that remain unfulfilled. Observe the gaps between where you are and where you want to be. By seeing the missing pieces we can start to set clear intentions.

What possible solutions exist for the areas of lack or dissatisfaction? If you were the master of the Universe, how could you meet that need?

Be playfully specific. How does the end result look, feel, sound, and smell? What color car, what type of home, what little things do you and a potential romantic partner both enjoy? When we practice that exercise, we start opening up and attracting new connections instead of ruminating on our perceived problems.

Create the space for alternatives to present themselves. Put yourself in a position to receive. What groups can you join? What talks can you go to? What podcasts can you listen to? What introductions can you make?

If you feel that wonderful synergy with someone, pursue it. Be open to being welcomed. You may well be the solution to someone else's dilemma. You just might be the person they have been looking for. Program your supercomputer to serve you in the way you choose.

—Amanda Hernandez

Life Wisdom:

___ ___ _____ ____

___ ___ ___ __ _____ __

___ ___ ___ _____

```
O  P  L  A  Y  F  U  L  L  Y  L  E  E  F  W  N
O  P  E  N  L  L  E  M  S  Y  O  J  N  E  T  H
E  M  S  M  H  T  I  R  O  G  L  A  C  B  I  L
E  S  A  H  S  I  E  V  R  E  S  L  N  G  N  T
E  H  S  S  E  A  T  R  S  Y  E  I  O  E  T  U
G  M  N  A  T  R  R  G  N  A  M  E  D  A  E  N
D  N  O  C  R  E  N  T  R  A  P  U  U  D  N  L
N  O  I  H  I  I  R  A  G  B  T  E  N  R  T  O
U  I  T  T  S  T  Y  I  N  I  A  I  I  E  I  O
O  T  C  S  C  M  N  G  T  D  A  Z  V  C  O  K
S  U  E  E  D  A  R  A  R  L  E  A  E  E  N  T
A  L  N  L  T  L  R  E  M  E  U  Z  R  I  S  Y
B  O  N  I  O  G  U  T  W  O  N  S  S  V  C  A
N  S  O  I  N  V  E  N  T  O  R  Y  E  E  A  T
T  N  C  R  A  M  A  N  D  A  P  A  S  R  C  T
```

Algorithms	Hernandez	Power
Alternatives	Home	Receive
Amanda	Imagination	Result
Attracting	Intentions	Romantic
Blessings	Inventory	Serve
Clear	Look	Smell
Connections	Master	Solution
Enjoy	Open	Sound
Feel	Partner	Synergy
Gratitude	Playfully	Universe

Reinvent Yourself Often

Who are you? Where are you going? Are others going with you? Are you an inspiration? What are you learning along the way as you travel from one opportunity to another in your life?

With each step we take, we choose a direction that allows us to define and refine who we are. We get stronger in confidence to our commitments as we move forward with conviction and integrity.

Each time we step beyond our comfort zones, we learn and grow. We avoid complacency and stagnation. We rebuild and reinvent ourselves. We see new pathways with an inner strength to pioneer a new roadmap for success. We become revitalized in the wonderment of unlimited possibilities. We are able to continually review and refine our vision. We can update our mission for leaving our positive mark on humanity. Engage. Emote. Energize.

Over the course of our life's journey, we build personal and professional relationships that impact our growth. The power of human connection makes our light take flight. Encountering success and opening the door for others to walk through is a soul-full and bonding experience. As we fulfill our dreams and goals, we light another's path.

Please keep sharing your gift of light to illuminate the path for others. As we mindfully stay true to ourselves, we find gratefulness, goodness in our lives, and peace. We nurture ourselves and are self-fulfilled in every new and improved version of who we are. You have the power to leave a legacy that is unique to you! Reinvent yourself often.

—*René Stern*

Life Wisdom:

— — — —   — — — —   — — — — —

— — — — — — — — —   — —   — — — — —   — — —

— — — —   — —   — — — —   — — — — —   — — — —

— — —   — — — —   — — — —   — — — —

```
I L L U M I N A T E E A H T S T
M N L I V E S L L N V T F O S R
P R S E W Y N E I O A I U R E A
R E U P G O G F R P G N S V N V
O N I Q I A E U E U B R I I D E
V E I S G R C L L I T T A N O L
E C R N E E A Y T O A R S H O N
D E E V N I N T P L E A U N G P
V D I R L I N O I T C I V N O C
G E E E H E W Z D O E T U S P D
W T M E V E E E E O N T I G R R
S E L N R D C I F V E T O E S T
H A I O N A Y O I U I A A M W I
L E L I E E V E N V L M R K E N
R O W P S U C C E S S S E N O Z
```

Conviction	Inspiration	Reinvent
Define	Legacy	Rene
Dreams	Lives	Review
Emote	Nurture	Revitalized
Engage	Path	Stern
Gift	Peace	Success
Goals	Pioneer	Travel
Goodness	Positive	Version
Illuminate	Power	Vision
Improved	Refine	Zones

The Sun and the Moon

Our cover is a symbol of wholeness through seeming opposites. The Sun and the Moon are opposites that exist together to create a whole. A whole day, a whole night, a whole range of human experience.

Our ancestors observed these celestial marvels keenly, and used that knowledge to understand and explain the working of their own lives. Life depended upon knowing the cycles of the Sun and Moon, to know when the flood times were, when to plant and harvest, and when to let things ripen. Knowledge of the cycles was recorded and passed along through generations. This essential wisdom, gathered through observation and meticulous record keeping, meant the difference between starvation and survival. It assured the continued thriving of civilization.

The Sun and Moon symbols appear on flags, in hieroglyphs, in ancient artwork and architecture, and are popular tattoos. They have long been part of the ritual and religious practices of different cultures.

The Sun rises during the day and sets during the night; this cycle is repetitive and constant. The Moon, on the other hand, stands for emotions and senses, since they are ever-changing and unpredictable, just like the planetary body. The Moon seemingly grows larger and smaller, waxes and wanes, and has different phases, just like our emotions. Each day is a different phase. Farmers have long planted by following the phases of the Moon.

MOON PHASES

The Moon reflects flexible, flowing, mystical (inward) energy, and supports intuition, process, wisdom, patience, and receptivity. The Sun emanates logical, initiating, magical (outward) energy, and rules action, tasks, knowledge, reason, and mathematics. We each carry our unique blend of solar and lunar energies within us. Our gender does not reflect which energy is predominant.

The symbol of yin and yang is a key. We humans are, like the symbol, comprised of opposing forces. Solar and lunar energies swirl within us in delicate balance. When we have too much of one energy or lack of another, we feel that imbalance.

To put lunar and solar energies into a nutshell: *do be do be do*. "Do" is solar; "be" is lunar.

To do and to be are two of the most basic verbs we use. They are described by Newton's Law of Inertia: a body in motion tends to stay in motion (*do*), and a body at rest tends to stay at rest (*be*). Are you a *do-er* or a *be-er*, or a *do be do be do-er?*

Our magical outer and mystical inner worlds both need nourishment. That balance helps us achieve and maintain optimum health. When we find ourselves out of balance, a quick whistle or hum of *do be do be do* can help us see where we need to adjust. Or at least make us laugh, and remember not to take ourselves so seriously.

We can positively impact our health by adding or subtracting *do* or *be* when we find our lives out of balance. Bring on the magic or disappear beyond the veil into the mystic. Contemplate your inner naval while engaging in a word search. Or hum a tune to lighten the mood. *Do be do be do.* Enjoy the magical mystical mix that is your extraordinary self!

We are one Earth under the Sun, the Moon, and the heavens above.

Duality into unity. Yin/yang. Feminine/masculine create the whole human. Right brain/left brain. Wholeness through opposites. Early Chinese writings described yin and yang more than three thousand years ago. Originally, they were not applied to the genders. The day is full of light and night is absent of light. The sunny side of the mountain is bright while the shady side lives in shadow.

No one is universally strong in all of the qualities of yin and yang. As humans seeking wholeness, we journey toward our goals. Knowing about these energies helps us in our quest. We nurture our strengths and grow where we are weak.

How and where and when are you sunny? How and where and when are you like the Moon? Are you balanced and in harmony with yourself? Most of us need a little help in this department. Use these two universal symbols to facilitate your own seeking of balance. *I need me some sunshine today! I'm feeling the Moon now and ebbing and flowing with my own tides.*

Symbols of all kinds can be powerful in our lives. Let these glorious heavenly bodies remind us of comfort and unity in the midst of daily life. Rising, setting, waxing, waning, in harmony with our own multiplicity of nature. The Moon reminds us it's only a phase. The Sun reminds us that not all days are shiny, yet the light will rise again. The Sun will come up tomorrow. Do be do be do.

41 The Power of Words

Have you ever stopped to really think about reading? What it is? How it's done? Reading really is our eyes scanning a piece of paper, or a screen, or a sign, or a building to find certain symbols which are arranged in a specific order. The power of these symbols, however small they might seem, is incredible. They allow us and others around us to understand what someone else is trying to communicate. And they don't have to be right there to tell us. They could be on the opposite side of the globe from where we are and still communicate with us.

A writer can create a whole new world for a reader to discover with magic, dragons, fairies, and giants, without either the writer or the reader ever physically leaving the non-magical world. The words are the tools in the box that we have to work with. The rest is up to us.

Words can make a reader feel sadness, hope, anger, joy, or confusion depending upon what their message is. They can relieve our sorrows and stresses, inspire us, and teach us things we didn't know about ourselves. In a non-magical world, words are perhaps the only true form of magic.

—Victoria DeVito

Life Wisdom:

_ _ _ _ _   _ _ _ _ _   _ _ · _ _ _   _ _ _ _ _ _ _,
_ _ _ _ _ _ _ _,   _ _ _ _ _ _,   _ _ _ _ _ _ _ _ _,
_ _ _   _ _ _ _ _ _ _ _ _ _ _

```
B O T O K D R A G O N S S O T
P P E W E N I U N L T P N O E
D O A W O R W O I L R I O L D
I W C I O R D S D A T L V H O
S E H T N L D W A M S U B E R
C R C Y R C R S E S S U G E D
O I O O H I R T R C I M D S F
V J W S T I D E R L A R T G A
E T A E R C E E D G O N A L I
R V R S F E E I I I A E L O R
I E E W I N N C N I B G S B I
P N D I O G A N G D P L E E E
S R G A L L S C I F I C E P S
N P E I E E L C P A P E R T I
I V E S S R R A S Y M B O L S
```

Allow	Inspire	Sign
Building	Joy	Small
Create	Magic	Specific
DeVito	Order	Symbols
Discover	Paper	Teach
Dragons	Power	Tools
Fairies	Reader	Victoria
Giants	Reading	Words
Globe	Relieve	World
Incredible	Screen	Writer

42 **Enjoy Augmenting Your Life**

We live in amazing times.

Our smart phones, tablets, and computers help us navigate our daily lives more effectively. They can show us a map of any place in the world. If we find ourselves chatting with a person from another culture, we can get a translation. We can see where they are from, including history, geography, and photographs.

We can write ourselves notes to remember holidays, meetings, and why we scheduled them. They then appear as a reminder at just the perfect time. Any question that we have can be answered to some degree by a quick search.

An internet camera can remind an Alzheimer's sufferer that they are looking at their child or spouse. We can chat over video with a friend or family member we may never see in person again. Some people are worried about all the cameras and loss of privacy. Technology is neutral, like a knife. It can be used be used for good or ill.

The extra abilities technology gifts us with augment our own intelligence and memory. Millions of programmers have spent careers coding artificial intelligences so all of us can have oodles of human knowledge in our pockets.

How will you use technology to enhance your life? The possibilities are endless. It's there for us to enjoy. Think about it the next time you reach for your phone, or ask Alexa or Siri or Google for directions or some information, or check to see who is ringing your doorbell. We really do live in amazing times.

—*Lisa Tansey*

Life Wisdom:

— — — — — — — — — — — — — —

— — — — — — — — — — — — — — — — —

— — — — — — — — — — — — — — — — —

```
E N A H A D N G O O G L E Y C
E Y O R N S E A R C H C R S S
O S R E T U P M O C N O Y E T
U E I R L I I A F E M N O L E
A R D E T H F Z G E R E J D L
F U Y I O Y L I M A F U N O B
U C G S V E L N C G H T E O A
P T O M I L R G H I E R W B T
S H L D E R O U N D A A I E R
M S O T I N I O T F O L U R A
A M N N A N T H O L I D A Y S
R I H A E N G Z C T U L I S A
T I C N G S S H I M T C E C H
A R E M A C A E A G I F T S N
O L T O G T S P Y A L E X A Y
```

Abilities	Enjoy	Neutral
Alexa	Family	Oodles
Amazing	Friend	Phones
Artificial	Gifts	Search
Augment	Google	Siri
Camera	Holidays	Smart
Chat	Intelligence	Tablets
Coding	Lisa	Tansey
Computers	Map	Technology
Culture	Memory	Video

Bake Your Unique Media Pie

Most of us use some kind of online media almost every day. From a CEO of a successful business to a grandmother staying connected to her family, we communicate online. How we manage that media can make the difference between being overwhelmed and distracted to taking advantage of the terrific technology tools available.

R - Remember your goals. A driven leader might want to increase impact while a working mom may want to make her community safer.

E - Media can engage, educate, entertain, and enlighten us. Remember that getting the most from online media happens when it is used in tandem with, but not replacing, offline resources.

C - Create the crust of your media pie by picking your foundation. An entrepreneur might want more potential clients visiting their website while a stay at home dad might want to attract more people to the community group he leads.

I - Brainstorm your media ingredients. From passing out Parent-Teacher Association flyers to engaging on social networking platforms to reaching your professional goals, options abound. Learn the ingredients you use.

P - Pick your favorite ingredients, prepare your unique media pie mix filling, and pour it into the crust of your foundation. Put it into the oven of life and bake. Test and adjust the recipe. It's an ongoing process of learning and reaching your goals.

E - Enjoy what you've created and appreciate the amazing access we have to connect. A recipe for success!

—*Gresham W. Harkless Jr.*

Life Wisdom:

___ ___ ___   ___ ___ ___   ___ ___ ___   ___ ___   ___ ___

___ ___ ___ ___   ___ ___ ___   ___ ___ ___ ___ ___

___ ___ ___   ___ ___   ___ ___ ___ ___

```
B A S L A O G E T A C U D E K
P O E T S U R C F I L L I N G
Y O N E M R O T S N I A R B O
U G U L T R M M E N E E E E D
I G R R I A P G I N N S N E
T N O A H N E R R E T J O G H
F I Y S N L E R E T S O U A C
T K E L S D R T C Y O Y R G U
R R P E I E M E H R S K C E O
G O N E C M N O M G L A E T L
G W N I P N A I T E I O S A A
L T P I O S A F S H D L N N D
S E E C M O M S X U E I N D V
E N T E R T A I N I B R A E A
D A D L E A D E R L M U E M S
```

Brainstorm	Enlighten	Media
Business	Entertain	Mix
Clients	Family	Mom
Connect	Filling	Networking
Create	Goals	Online
Crust	Grandmother	Pie
Dad	Gresham	Pour
Educate	Harkless	Recipe
Engage	Ingredients	Resources
Enjoy	Leader	Tandem

44 Be a Forward Thinker

We live in a society that demands instant gratification. Fast food, quarterly stock reports, and internet shopping; all of these things encourage us to make decisions in the moment without regard for the future. We have moved so far from the native tradition of thinking seven generations ahead that we rarely even consider seven days ahead. However, we can be the change we want to see in the world by being forward thinkers.

Do you feel like sitting on your couch every evening and weekend bingeing Netflix and eating junk food? Me too! What will that do for our long-term health goals? Want to indulge in a new gadget that popped up on your Facebook page? Me too! What will that do for our finances when it is time to pay the mortgage or rent? Such pesky questions!

On a more global level, do we want to continue extracting fossil fuels from the Earth and creating pollution, or move to renewable energy? The easy choice is often not the right one.

Consider being a forward thinker. Before making any decision, think how it will affect you and your tribe in a year, or ten years, or twenty-five years. If we all live more conscientiously, together we *can* change the world. Let's make a future we all want, together.

—*Valerie Costa*

Life Wisdom:

— — — — — — — — — — — — — — — — —
— — — — — — — — — — — — — — — — —
— — — — — — — — — — — —

```
W  S  E  C  N  A  N  I  F  O  R  W  A  R  D
E  O  E  C  O  R  E  A  G  A  D  G  E  T  T
N  C  N  E  I  O  U  T  O  G  E  T  H  E  R
E  I  E  O  S  D  R  F  T  N  A  T  S  N  I
R  E  A  K  I  L  L  U  E  V  I  T  A  N  R
G  T  S  T  C  T  E  R  V  A  L  E  R  I  E
Y  Y  Y  U  E  O  A  V  O  R  E  E  V  R  N
H  E  R  Y  D  T  T  C  E  W  D  A  U  O  E
T  Y  W  I  I  T  H  S  I  L  E  T  I  G  W
L  A  B  O  L  G  V  E  R  F  U  T  N  O  A
A  Y  N  A  T  S  O  C  C  F  I  A  H  A  B
E  S  H  C  U  O  C  O  I  D  H  T  C  L  L
H  N  E  V  E  S  E  W  A  C  E  M  A  S  E
Y  K  S  E  P  A  K  R  T  R  I  B  E  R  E
R  E  K  N  I  H  T  S  H  O  P  P  I  N  G
```

Change	Generations	Seven
Costa	Global	Shopping
Couch	Goals	Society
Decision	Gratification	Stock
Easy	Health	Thinker
Energy	Instant	Together
Finances	Level	Tradition
Forward	Native	Tribe
Future	Pesky	Valerie
Gadget	Renewable	World

45   Gifts for Our Children

Having children is one of the great responsibilities in life. How we raise our children, and what we teach them, not only shapes their lives but also affects the future collective mindset of all of humanity. It is no insignificant undertaking!

I was fortunate to have my first child later in life. This is because by that time I had become very clear about my own values and belief systems. I was aware that she would be impressionable, and would learn about life by watching how I lived mine. I wanted to parent consciously, aware of the lessons I would teach. Be kind. It's okay to make mistakes. Trust yourself. You live in an abundant Universe. Create!

Children learn by what we tell them verbally, but even more so by what they see us do and say. Conscious parenting is about being aware of what we want to teach our children and then mindfully demonstrating those lessons with our words and actions. It means paying attention to our behavior, recognizing that our choices become teaching tools for our children.

Conscious parenting provides us with the opportunity to delve deeply into our own thought patterns and beliefs, deciding what we want to perpetuate, and what we want to prevent from being imprinted on our children and on future generations. We are teaching our children, yet they are also teaching us, reflecting back to us the values and belief systems we have imparted. Being a parent is not only a great responsibility, but also a tremendous gift of self-awareness and love.

—*Paula Wansley*

Life Wisdom:

___ ___ ___ _____ ___ ___ _____ ___

___ ___ _____ ___

_____ __ _____ _____ __

___ _____

```
O U T R S D R O W W O R W F D S
A N E R D L I H C N D A U D G A
S H R P U C T I O O N T E E N S
E N C A E S A R L S U L N T E T
K H R A E R T E L R V E L N E S
A S A E E L P E E E R O N I S A
T T U C T T Y E C A N D T R G I
S N N A T T E N T I O N F P T R
I E I A A I A I I U E S W M O E
M R V L D W O P V V A E P I T A
A A E O S N A N E A S T V A L S
A P R V S L U R S L O A E U T D
N G S E T O P B E U H R A F N O
U T E S D N I M A E C P I I R C
H I L F E I L E B S D G K R E N
```

Abundant	Future	Patterns
Actions	Generations	Paula
Attention	Gifts	Perpetuate
Aware	Imprinted	Prevent
Behavior	Kind	Teach
Belief	Learn	Trust
Children	Love	Universe
Collective	Mindset	Values
Create	Mistakes	Wansley
Delve	Parent	Words

46 Boost Your Health and Vitality

Want to improve your health and indoor air quality? Reduce allergies? Have more energy? Sleep better? Help save the planet? And have fun doing it? Create a fully organic and chemical-free lifestyle.

It's not easy. Getting started can be overwhelming and complex. It can be tempting to give up before seeing some of the remarkable benefits. However, solution-based small steps make this lifestyle change easy, simple, and fun.

What's the best way to start? Bring organic, chemical-free products home one step and one item at a time. As the old familiar brands run out, replace them with those that are healthier. This method eliminates overwhelm and prioritizes upgrading the things we use most frequently.

Lifestyle change doesn't start and end in one day. It's a consistent and conscious choice. Start small. Allow flexibility. It's okay to backtrack a bit and then continue forward. Keep going.

Take. One. Step. At. A. Time.

One day you'll look back and realize just how far you've come. You'll be happy and proud knowing that your organic, chemical-free household is good for your kids, pets, family, and visitors. What an amazing feeling that is.

—*Angela Cummings*

Life Wisdom:

__ __ __ __ __ __ __   __ __ __   __ __ __ __ __ __ __   __ __

__ __ __ __   __ __ __ __   __ __ __   __ __ __ __   __ __

__ __ __ __   __ __ __ __ __ __

```
Y D S U P G S O L U T I O N Y
S O R R C A K I D S C A P T G
A O O A P O H D E O H N R R R
E G T R I L N E N T O G O A E
Y H I N E R A S A E M E U T N
Q T S U U P C N I L E L D S E
A L I F I I L T E S T A Y O S
F Y V L O O U A C T T H R T L
S I F U A E A I C C N E I D I
Y D S H O T N M H E E F N E M
L P N B Y A I O G L E O I T P
I E N A G G I V P N S T E P R
M E O R R C R M E Y P P A H O
A L O G E B I B A T S O O B V
F S N I C S S G N I M M U C E
```

Air	Energy	Pets
Angela	Family	Planet
Benefits	Fun	Proud
Boost	Good	Replace
Brands	Happy	Simple
Choice	Health	Sleep
Conscious	Home	Solution
Consistent	Improve	Start
Cummings	Kids	Visitors
Easy	Organic	Vitality

How to Save the World

At heart, people are good. Most everyone wants to save the world.

It's easy to imagine our ideal world in our mind's eye. It's easy to believe our approach to life will work for everyone.

We think that if we could only get people to listen to us and agree, the world would change for the better.

It's tempting to try and impose our beliefs on others. Yet we need to understand that everyone's vision of utopia is unique. Forcing our vision on others builds resistance, anger, and fear in them and us. People easily become defensive. Like wild animals backed into a corner, their survival instinct kicks in. Instead of growling and snarling, we humans judge, criticize, and verbally berate each other. This is our attempt to protect ourselves from a perceived attack. It all happens under the radar of our conscious awareness.

This invasive dominate-and-overpower approach to saving the world is common in society. We are inundated with messages about how to think, be, and act.

In reality, the exact opposite approach is what works. The steps are simple. We shift our focus away from the world and look within. There, we receive messages that work for us without power plays. This allows inner peace into our hearts and minds.

Like magic, life becomes a joy and a pleasure. If we each look within and save ourselves, we will save the world.

—*Jennifer Whitacre*

Life Wisdom:

— — — —   — — — —   — — — — —   — — — — —   — —

— — — — —   — — — — —   — — —

— — — — — — — — —   — — — — — — —

```
F  T  I  N  D  E  R  K  O  O  L  I  Y  O
E  F  U  R  S  E  G  A  S  S  E  M  I  D
V  I  E  P  C  A  P  N  Y  L  W  A  O  R
E  H  L  E  L  P  A  M  A  O  D  G  I  B
I  S  I  Y  R  E  P  G  A  H  J  I  D  H
L  V  G  O  O  I  A  E  R  G  C  N  E  E
E  I  A  N  G  W  I  S  A  E  I  E  A  A
B  C  S  E  U  Q  I  N  U  C  E  C  L  R
H  W  P  T  R  E  N  N  I  R  E  T  U  T
D  O  R  H  E  I  N  T  C  N  E  A  T  N
L  R  O  N  D  N  C  A  D  I  I  S  O  M
R  K  T  C  O  A  T  V  E  H  R  I  P  I
O  J  E  N  N  I  F  E  R  T  S  I  I  N
W  N  C  G  H  S  A  V  E  I  Y  O  A  D
U  R  T  W  S  E  Y  E  V  W  E  L  F  S
```

Act	Jennifer	Receive
Agree	Joy	Save
Approach	Listen	Shift
Believe	Look	Unique
Change	Magic	Utopia
Eye	Messages	Vision
Heart	Minds	Whitacre
Ideal	Peace	Within
Imagine	Pleasure	Work
Inner	Protect	World

48   Art with a Purpose

Art is an excellent way to express our thoughts and feelings. Even if you don't consider yourself artistic, you still can make something that conveys your inner ideas.

Don't be intimidated. There are no limitations. No boundaries. Your inner child probably already knows what it wants to express and how it wants to express it. Art is not like math or science, where the outcome has to be exact. We are not being graded or compared. Feel free to design what you want because there are absolutely no mistakes in art. Whew!

We each get to decide what our art means. We get to explore what we feel and share the significance according to our own interpretation. "I made it to be this way" can be our default explanation.

Our lives are actually an art piece, a creation of our own imaginations. Art is a powerful tool that can help us visually identify where we are now and where we want to be in the future. We get to mold, color, texturize, and signify what we want ourselves to be.

To get started on your unique masterpiece, consider making a vision board with your future life as the theme. Ask yourself, what does my imagined life look like? Be specific. Be detailed. What am I wearing? What am I doing? Who am I with? How am I feeling being there?

Visualize who you want to be. Express it in your art project. Make it real. Allow your inner artist to help you envision and create your best life.

—*Tamlin Allbritten*

Life Wisdom:

__ __ __ __   __ __ __ __   __ __   __   __ __ __ __ __

__ __ __ __ __ __,   __ __ __ __ __ __   __

__ __ __ __ __ __ __ __ __

```
I D E N T I F Y E E M E H T Y
G N I L E E F S V R E N N I D
O U T R L I O I E R O L P X E
F E I E S P S S T H G U O H T
C E Z I R U T X E T W O L L A
I A B U A P T A M L I N L A I
F N P L V C R P O W E R F U L
I K I D I O S E Y T N E C A E
C Z F E S L S N T F O L E V D
E V U S U O E I A A I D O R S
P I T I A R R C R L T N L O F
S S U G L B P E A A A I G O T
T I R N L E X A M E E A O I M
A O E L Y S E T E R R R R N S
P N A I S Y E V N O C E C T E
```

Allbritten	Feeling	Signify
Allow	Free	Specific
Art	Future	Tamlin
Color	Identify	Texturize
Conveys	Inner	Theme
Creation	Interpretation	Thoughts
Design	Mold	Tool
Detailed	Powerful	Vision
Explore	Purpose	Visualize
Express	Real	Visually

49 The Work Is Great, So Do It

There is a common thread to all great passions in the world. There is the yearning we have to achieve. There is the focus of doing the work. Then there is the dedication to the path.

All of these elements have helped me to think, act, and speak differently to better realize who I am and who I will become. I started on a spiritual path that has opened my eyes to many things. I have learned how my thoughts, words, and actions have held me back. I have learned to cultivate an internal peace, to be calm and focused.

Through martial arts I learned physical discipline, honor, and mutual respect. My practice regimen enabled me to realize how I can stretch, become stronger, and be true to myself.

Through music, I learned I had more capability than I realized. I learned to sing, play, and work with others in creative ways. I also learned this was my calling, and that without it I would suffer. My path has allowed me to manifest the teachers, friends, and relationships that have helped me become who I am today.

All of these practices take time, effort, dedication, discipline, and hard work. Each practice helps to build a foundation. Some of the elements that help to create balance in life are passion, yearning, work, physicality, movement, creativity, and community. We each have a great work to become our best selves. Do it!

—*Tony Connors*

Life Wisdom:

— — — — — — — — — — — — — — — — — — — —

— — — — — — — — — — — — — — — — — — — —

— — — — — — — — — — — — — —

```
D N O I S S A P T C O N E O T
B E F F O R T S O A E N N G A
H O N O R O D F N L I E N Y L
C O M M U N I T Y L M I A D A
W R A I E N O D P I S L T E U
O O P I W O O I G N P R Y D T
K E R R H C C E T G A E R I U
D F L K A S R E N A A O U C M
G H A E I C B T H R D O L A U
E H N D M E T A N C A N N T S
R T R E N E C I L H T I U I I
O A E M W G N A C A F E R O C
E P T I A G T T E E N Y R N F
O U N T C A R E S P E C T T N
B E I G R E A T E A C H E R S
```

Balance	Great	Practice
Calling	Honor	Regimen
Community	Internal	Respect
Connors	Manifest	Sing
Dedication	Music	Stretch
Discipline	Mutual	Teachers
Effort	Passion	Time
Elements	Path	Tony
Foundation	Peace	Work
Friends	Play	Yearning

50 Find Your Purpose

After many years focused on setting and achieving goals, I sensed a feeling of dissatisfaction. Is this all there is? I enjoyed the work that I did, but it wasn't enough. What was the purpose of it all? Not long after, I went to a meeting where the presenter shared his story of failure, bankruptcy, and breakthrough. It was an *aha* moment for me. He talked about how nothing he had accomplished had any meaning until he found his personal purpose.

Finding my purpose wasn't easy. Two years of reading and researching information didn't get me any closer. Then I remembered the presenter's suggestion that I think about my memorial service. What would I want people in all the different areas of my life to say about me? What was my legacy? It felt uncomfortable, but I was determined.

I considered my business associates, spiritual group, and friends. Then I thought of my family, which was the hardest part, until I pictured my eleven-year-old grandson. The realization that I had already influenced his life opened my eyes. I became aware that I was already guiding people to help them see and recognize their potential.

It isn't often that you know for sure you have made a difference. Then one day someone walks up to you in a parking lot and says they remember you from twenty-eight years ago and how much you positively impacted their life. It is that feeling, that somehow my presence a long time ago inspired someone. I may never know how. That's the day I discovered my purpose. This is how I want to be remembered!

—*Barbara Eldridge*

Life Wisdom:

— — — —   — — — — —   — — — — — — —

— — — — — — —   — —   — — — — — —   — — —

— — —   — — — —   —   — — — — — — — — —

— — — —

```
F  I  I  N  S  P  I  R  E  D  N  S  D  Y  P  F  B
E  C  N  E  U  L  F  N  I  B  O  P  U  R  R  R  A
G  P  S  P  E  R  S  F  A  O  N  I  A  L  E  I  N
D  R  L  E  P  U  F  R  R  P  O  R  S  A  S  E  K
I  E  E  T  T  E  B  F  O  C  H  I  K  I  E  N  R
R  S  O  O  R  A  A  F  S  E  H  T  Y  T  N  D  U
D  E  T  E  R  M  I  N  E  D  H  U  C  N  T  S  P
L  N  N  A  I  N  A  C  S  R  F  A  A  E  E  L  T
E  C  O  L  D  H  G  S  O  A  E  L  G  T  R  A  C
E  E  Y  W  A  N  E  U  I  S  Y  O  E  O  U  I  Y
P  A  R  K  I  N  G  L  O  T  S  L  L  P  I  R  V
E  A  F  D  I  H  U  P  S  G  R  A  N  D  S  O  N
U  L  I  S  E  R  R  E  F  D  E  T  C  A  P  M  I
I  U  U  L  E  U  Y  L  L  R  E  B  M  E  M  E  R
G  B  P  E  P  E  D  L  I  F  S  L  A  O  G  M  E
```

Aha	Failure	Inspired
Associates	Family	Legacy
Bankruptcy	Find	Memorial
Barbara	Friends	Parking Lot
Breakthrough	Goals	Potential
Business	Grandson	Presence
Determined	Guiding	Presenter
Difference	Help	Purpose
Eldridge	Impacted	Remember
Eyes	Influence	Spiritual

The Power of Purpose

Why are you here on Earth? Do you know your purpose? Do you have one? Are you pursuing it daily and avidly, or do you have a little niggling sense that there is something *more* for you in this life?

Purpose gives meaning to our lives so we can live a meaningful life. Our purpose is our inner navigation system, daily motivator, personal coach, and cheerleader all rolled into one. It gives us the strength, determination, and clarity to bring our past, present, and future into focus. It helps us make good decisions that fit with our goals and what we really want. We are each on Earth for a special purpose. What is yours? Only you can name it.

Having a purposeful life is good for us. It protects against cognitive decline in older adults and contributes to overall health and well-being for all ages. An overwhelming three-quarters of people over sixty-five have multiple chronic health conditions. Recent evidence finds that a high sense of purpose is associated with positive health outcomes among older adults. Lower levels of purpose were significantly associated with higher numbers of chronic conditions. Childhood adversity may restrict our search for purpose in life. Don't let that stop you now!

We need to pursue our purpose as though our life depends on it, because it does.

Adding a dose of purpose can transform an existence of loneliness, depression, and futility to a meaningful life of well-being, happiness, joy, and community. Even dogs love having a purpose. Children need purpose and thrive when focused on a task they understand that brings meaning.

The most basic question everyone faces in life is *Why am I here? What is my purpose?* Some say we need to look within, at our interests, talents, skills, dreams, and drives. Others say we need to ask a Higher Power about our eternal purpose. One of our human quests is to do whatever we can to find it. *Do be do be do.*

Purpose is not something that others can choose for us. It is something we each have the pleasure, privilege, and responsibility to discover for ourselves. It emerges from an exploration of what we value most. It's one of those questions a Google search can't answer. Though it's not a bad place to start to research ideas.

When we realize that each person has their own unique purpose, different yet equal from our own, it makes it easier to support each other and collaborate. Competition is no longer about others. It becomes about bettering ourselves each and every day.

As long as our purpose fills us with passion, it can be anything from quiet and private to public and global. It's what gets the juices flowing, touches the heart, and makes a difference. Knowing our purpose helps us define our goals and can make life much more enjoyable and graceful. It's why we get up in the morning.

Still searching? Not sure? Some find these questions helpful when seeking their purpose.

What do you value most? What brings you joy? What fills you with enthusiasm? How do you want to make a difference? What do you want to be known and remembered for?

When the answers come, write them down. Start and end each day by reading your purpose aloud. Adjust as needed. Sometimes purpose takes fine tuning. Sometimes purpose changes over time.

Having a purpose translates to better well-being for each of us, our families, and the world. It gives a whole new meaning to doing something *on purpose*.

Once we know our purpose, we can birth it into our lives through our thoughts, words, and actions every single day. It can also function as a benchmark, when we review our day, our year, our lives.

Purposeful choice transcends the daily grind of living and promotes joy, moments of happiness, and contentment. It's never too late. Chances are excellent that purpose has been there all along. Breathe it into life.

Breath Connections and Cycles

The wise doctor or midwife encourages. She tells the laboring woman, "Just connect to your breath. One breath, one push at a time. You've got this!" We enter the life-cycle with a breath. Seconds after that miraculous first inspiration, we learn about connections through the touch of the midwife or doctor's hands. We may breathe a cry at the shock of hearing sound disconnected from the watery womb. We taste mother's milk. Mama and baby breathe together. Our parents breathe and cry in joy. Gasping with pain and pleasure, we all breathe connected breaths.

Sharing breaths, we laugh, explore, and discover how to communicate desires. We breathe together and grow. We experience play, work, and perhaps be enthused enough to enter a connected relationship with the one who takes our breath away!

Taking profoundly deep breaths, we dive into making a family. This includes loss. Graced, we witness a cherished loved one take their last precious inspiration, then release it into the final exhalation of silence. And we breathe in the air of their last breath, forever connected to the cycle of the breaths of our ancestry.

Words uttered or sung are preceded by a breath. Precious chances to create new beginnings. What desires will be born of your breaths? Take them not for granted, for they are inspirationally filled by you and those we all breathe with in connection. Breathe in. Step out with courage. Design your unique identity, one breath, one step, one cycle at a time. Breathe in your connectedness. We've got this, together.

—*Shelley Hines*

Life Wisdom:

__ __ __ __ __ __ __ __ __ __ __ __ __ __ __ __ __ __

__ __ __ __ __ __ __ __ __ __ __ __ __ __ __ __ __

__ __ __ __ __ __ __ __ __ __ __ __ __ __ __ __ __ __-

__ __ __ __

```
T A Y K E A E P L E A S U R E
M O E R M E C G R N T C T O D
S L O T C W N N D E Y O B E W
C O U R A G E U N C C R S E A
H I N E S C L S L O E I F N D
E I R Y N S I E N A G I O P I
R R E O O A S N T N W N Y U D
I T E N T J E H U D J Y R E S
S U O L U C A R I M E O T T B
H Y A G T B O M R L M G S A M
E E A I E T H D L K R O E E O
D O O M B T W E C A F S C R W
E N I A A O H O C L F C N C A
S L B I R S H E S E C N A H C
K Y R G R S D E R Y R E T A W
```

Air	Cry	Miraculous
Ancestry	Cycles	Pleasure
Baby	Design	Precious
Breath	Doctor	Shelley
Chances	Graced	Shock
Cherished	Grow	Silence
Communicate	Hines	Sung
Connections	Joy	Together
Courage	Midwife	Watery
Create	Milk	Womb

52   **Word Wise**

Words have power. Intrinsically they have a tone, a vibration, a resonance that has varying degrees of impact on those who hear them. The power is always greatest when it resonates at the same frequency as the person who receives it. Do you ever hear a word or phrase that you've heard many times before, but suddenly it all makes sense? That's because you and the words are on the same frequency, and that's when the real magic happens!

So, let's not only use our words, but *choose* our words. Being word wise is a form of mindfulness that gives us strength and empowers us to authentically move towards our highest good.

Here's an example from my own experience. I have heard and read during my life's journey that it's important to learn to let go of issues that may be troubling us. We are instructed to surrender to the power of the Universe to let our good come to us. I believe in the concepts. Yet within me, the words *let go* and *surrender* were equal to *give up* and *quit*, a passive approach that I couldn't quite ever buy into. Instead I started using the word *release*, and what a difference it's made! To me, release is something that I can actively do and control. It empowers me and creates a shift in my attitude that the other words were not accomplishing.

The words that empower you might be different, and that's great! Just be sure to mindfully choose those that truly resonate with you. The right words provide the inner harmony, strength, and clarity to make all of life sing.

—*Bertha Edington*

Life Wisdom:

— — — — — — —   — — —   — — — — —

— — — — — — — — — —   — — —   — — — —

— — — — — — — — — — —   — —   —

— — — — — — —   — — — — — —

```
T A T T I T U D E C G H F R O O
C C U T S I S N G O R W R E C S
O I A T O U T R O E I W E L H I
N O G P H N R D S S R D Q E O N
S O B A M E E O E D E L U A O G
I B T E M I N D F U L N E S S E
R A S G R A G T T E O L N E E Y
A N T D N T T W I I I T C H C E
O Y P C N I H S T C Y C Y I T S
O U E S I A D A E T A N O S E R
N E C N R S R E I R S L E I S E
S A N M R B P R E O W H L E A V
R E O F I U A W T H G I R Y R I
R N C V U L O T F I H S L A H N
Y C T I C P O J H D R O W N P U
```

Attitude	Highest	Resonate
Authentically	Impact	Right
Bertha	Inner	Shift
Choose	Journey	Sing
Clarity	Magic	Strength
Concepts	Mindfulness	Tone
Edington	Phrase	Universe
Frequency	Power	Vibration
Good	Release	Wise
Harmony	Resonance	Word

53 **Be Magical**

You are magical.

This is one truth about marvelous humanity. We are scintillating creatures. The secret is in how we access ourselves. We need to crack our own code. Find out what makes us tick. Access our own magic. There are sparkles inside us that need nourishing. That nourishment comes from being seen.

Being seen helps us feel supported. Often, we need to see ourselves first. There is a luminous light inside. This spark of precious light is a firework of joy. We are contagious beings who spread our light to each other. We have mysteries within the walls of our cells. These mysteries are talking to us now. They are saying there is a lightshow to enjoy.

Nothing out there is going to give us the key to ourselves. You are the key. You are the code. You are the magic. This is exciting. Right now, inside our cells, our microscopic mitochondria are busy at work. What are they doing? They are creating energy out of thin air. They are catching streams of light from the Universe. What a marvel is unfolding within us now. Our mitochondria are weaving energy from the cosmos into our cells.

We are constantly converting energy from outside to form magic within. Let us embody this new frequency of light for all. What if we begin to unleash it in new ways? As we celebrate the magic in others, ours grows too. Seeing, supporting, and nourishing each other's sparkle, we are magnificent co-creators with the All!

—*Alessandra Gilioli*

Life Wisdom:

— — — — — — — — — — — — — — — — —

— — — — — — — — — — — — — — — — — — —

— — — — — — — — — — — — — —

— — — — — — — — —

```
W E Y C H T U R T L E V R A M E N
A D D R O E P E S R E V I N U E Y
E O O O W S A E R U F U L G E O S
T C B P A C M L R K O S N S J O F
A N M L I R Y O E G N I V A E W L
R S E A N A S G S S T F C I N U Y
B S L C I C T T I A S E C E M G C
E E K I I K E O L L S A M I R I R
L C R G C F R L L I I G N E H P E
E C A A T M I T O C H O N D R I A
C A P M S T E N H I U E L F R T T
I N S G N I S N G S T O T I N A U
E W E I S L L E C A X P K I R E R
S Y C N E U Q E R F M S I E C O E
N S U P P O R T T E R C E S Y K S
```

Access	Frequency	Precious
Alessandra	Gilioli	Scintillating
Celebrate	Joy	Secret
Cells	Key	Seen
Code	Luminous	Sparkle
Cosmos	Magical	Support
Crack	Magnificent	Tick
Creatures	Marvel	Truth
Embody	Mitochondria	Universe
Energy	Mysteries	Weaving

54   Take a Labyrinth Journey

Either in your imagination or with your physical body, enter the labyrinth. This particular one has a center circle. The goal is to reach the center, then walk your way back out. Chalk lines in the dirt create this mysterious maze.

Begin the journey, placing one foot in front of the other. Might as well relax and have fun with it. Soften the gaze and deepen the breath. It becomes a walking meditation, one foot mindfully in front of the other. Slow down. Become present. Listen to the sounds around you. Are there birds? Feel the breeze, or the stillness.

Suddenly, you are a mere chalk line away from the center, your goal! You feel so close. In another short moment, a few steps, you find yourself way out on the furthest edge. You couldn't be any farther away from your goal. The reality is that you are in fact closer to your goal now than when you were one chalk line away. You have only moved forward. You are further along the path.

The Universe works in a zig zag fashion. Life is not linear. Trust. With steady, forward steps, and intention, we will walk one day into our future goal. It may be just around the corner. Keep steady, breathe, and relax.

Allow yourself to be pleasantly surprised when you realize that you have made it to the center. It is as if the labyrinth walked you to your goal, rather than you walking the labyrinth. Wise labyrinth. Wise you.

—Kim Kinjo

Life Wisdom:

_ _

_ _

_ _

```
I P R E S E N T M E A G Z I P
S B I R D S N E H E Y I S A Y
C L O U M R G T L E G O T N O
M E O A L E A B N C U H C O S
E I N W E E D R I N R H N I P
G S K T R A U I D S A I T T E
F H I B E O T S T L H E C N T
A K T W J R C I K A E N T E S
S I G N I K L A W B T E R T N
H N R A I L T H E R G I R N E
I J T H N R A N O E F O O I T
O O U E T I Y N T E M O A N S
N H S E G D E B E Z Z A O L I
D S I T S U R T A E S A Z T L
T E Z I L A E R A L N C G E E
```

Birds	Intention	Realize
Breathe	Journey	Slow
Breeze	Kim	Sounds
Center	Kinjo	Steps
Chalk	Labyrinth	Stillness
Circle	Listen	Trust
Edge	Maze	Walking
Fashion	Meditation	Wise
Foot	Path	Zag
Goal	Present	Zig

See the World

Travel is always more than just the outward journey; it's also a journey inward. A transformational journey into ourselves. That's the beauty of travel, we get to see ourselves in a new light. Exploring our beautiful planet and humanity in a conscious, authentic, and experiential way is life-changing.

We are all explorers at heart; we long to travel deeper and go beyond. Travelers crave mystery, enlightenment, and an open door to transformation. We are individualistic seekers, yearning to live our own truth to the fullest. Underneath it all, the allure of travel is not that we get to see new places, but that we get to see ourselves.

We each share a global soul. What separates us from those in distant lands is less than what unites us all as explorers here on Earth. See the world, and find our differences are just illusions. The most powerful moments happen when we connect with someone without a common language, or when we trust a stranger. We begin to see the familiar behind the exotic. We get that first glimpse behind our own mask.

Globetrotting brings confidence, insights, and opens new horizons. The biggest secret? All the wisdom we will find on our adventures was already inside of us before we set out. Travel transforms us so it appears right before our eyes. Seeing the world is a wondrous journey back to our heart's truth.

—Pauliina Parris

Life Wisdom:

_ _ _ _ _ _ _ _ _ _ _ _ _ _ _ _ _ _

_ _ _ _ _ _ _ _ _ _ _ _ _ _ _ _ _ _ _ _

_ _ _ _ _ _ _ _ _ _ _ _ _ _ _

```
H P A U L I I N A M I N P S I
M O D S I W D F U U L L E N P
H A R T R T A V T E A R S A T
L E S I L I R N H N U I R R W
S A A K Z A R A E T G R U D A
Y E N R U O J T N H I T N D C
T S E D T O N E T S H U T I S
U P D K S H V S I W F A T R U
A M T R E D E R C D C O E O O
E I D S A R R R L N X R R N I
B L S L U W S A U E O N E M C
C G T E R R N S W L V M Y O S
U T O Y Y O T I P T L A M O N
U R G L O E W X B A U A R O O
L S O U T C E N N O C O L T C
```

Adventures	Eyes	Parris
Allure	Glimpse	Pauliina
Authentic	Heart	Planet
Beauty	Horizons	Seekers
Common	Insights	Transforms
Connect	Inward	Travel
Conscious	Journey	Trust
Earth	Lands	Truth
Exotic	Mask	Wisdom
Explorers	Outward	World

56   Oneness Is Our Future

There is no more important lesson in the world today than that of oneness. Oneness is the idea that we are all connected together, that there is really only one collective unity of all beings. We are all interdependent. As we face the future of our struggling planet with its rapidly changing dynamics, we stare into the face of possible loss of life on Earth as we know it.

Now, more than ever, it is essential we bring our awareness to focus on our oneness. Oneness is no longer a nice idea but a core value, an essential mindset we need to rapidly adopt if we are to rescue our world.

We must work together, as one, to make the changes that will save our planet and restore our humanity. If we each commit to living in oneness, seeing all of us as a single global soul, we would be unable to make war on each other. If we recognize the absolute perfection of our shared experience, we would see no political differences. We would embrace our unity rather than leaning on those things we believe make us separate.

We are one. When we adopt a belief in oneness, it underlies our decisions and helps us to survive and thrive through the challenges ahead. We are in this together. All for one and one for all!

—*Karen Stuth*

Life Wisdom:

__ __   ____   _____

_____   __   ____   _____

_____   __   ____   ____

```
I P T O G E T H E R O T S E R
S N L A S O U L U T H E E G R
C T P A L A T E F M V U L H E
A O U E N L R T S I A E V A S
P A R T R E D E T C E N N O C
T C E E H F T C O B E L I E F
E M B R A C E H F O U A R T D
S T S S H L F C R A R W E D Y
D S P U L K U U T I E A E R N
N X E O C V A N T I V R V E A
I P C N D O A R I U O E I S M
M E R I E A F L E T R N V C I
E N C E W N E A U N Y E R U C
R E A R T H O E O E N S U E S
G L O B A L A I T N E S S E E
```

Adopt	Essential	Rescue
All	Focus	Restore
Awareness	Future	Save
Belief	Global	Soul
Collective	Humanity	Stuth
Connected	Karen	Survive
Core	Mindset	Thrive
Dynamics	Oneness	Together
Earth	Perfection	Unity
Embrace	Planet	Value

57 Full-Spectrum Blessings

For generations, the Western world's concept of "deity" has been almost entirely male, and primarily an old male at that. Spiritually powerful women, where allowed, were only tolerated as saints under the control of others. Holy mothers were allowed to deliver a god, like a package they were entrusted to carry. Women's spiritual contributions were not given any credit. Yet, we arose from numerous cultures that were rich in goddesses: Celtic, Native American, Minoan, Norse, Egyptian, Indigenous, Greek, Roman, Asian, and African, among many others.

One of the most enduring and influential embodiments of the divine feminine is Isis, the Lady of Ten Thousand names. This benevolent goddess sprang from the dark earth of Egypt and then spread her wings over the world. Temples arose for her throughout the Greek and Roman world. The trade routes carried her influence into India, China, and beyond. Isis' presence and message of passionate love, unwavering persistence, and creative self-reliance have empowered countless worshippers, liberated oppressed women and men, and served as an icon of all forms of nurturing limitless abundance, Divine Love, and Sacred Union.

When the divine feminine and the sacred masculine are brought together, the entire spectrum of human union can be experienced and treasured. True fulfillment and happiness are possible when both aspects are recognized. All come together in a fluid balance of mingled energies and magic.

—deTraci Regula

Life Wisdom:

— —————— —— ———————
———————— ———— ——— ———————
———————— ——— ——————— ————
——————— ——

```
S  G  N  I  S  S  E  L  B  A  R  I  R  E  S
D  I  V  I  N  E  S  O  F  B  O  N  A  C  A
G  E  N  T  E  D  I  R  N  U  M  P  H  A  C
E  R  T  D  R  M  I  F  E  N  A  I  S  E  R
C  E  E  R  I  C  A  G  T  D  N  I  L  H  E
A  N  V  E  A  A  R  G  E  A  A  T  M  O  D
N  I  I  N  K  C  N  N  I  N  I  Y  W  I  T
O  N  T  H  T  H  I  S  O  C  O  M  E  D  I
I  I  A  V  I  L  G  R  N  E  U  U  S  E  F
N  M  N  C  U  N  S  E  N  R  M  Y  S  A  L
U  E  E  C  I  E  A  A  T  S  N  L  E  T  D
S  F  S  W  A  R  O  C  I  C  R  O  D  P  E
H  A  P  P  I  N  E  S  S  D  M  H  D  Y  A
M  L  E  W  I  P  I  M  E  V  O  L  O  G  I
T  H  I  M  S  N  M  E  A  A  L  U  G  E  R
```

Abundance	Feminine	Masculine
African	Goddess	Minoan
American	Greek	Native
Asian	Happiness	Norse
Blessings	Holy	Regula
Celtic	India	Roman
China	Indigenous	Sacred
DeTraci	Isis	Spectrum
Divine	Love	Union
Egypt	Magic	Wings

58 The Lamp of Love

As our soul's divine impulses come firing,
love's presence moves freely,
uplifting within heart's soulful existence.

Fueling purified openings into blissful joy,
love makes its eventual merge as Divine Oneness.
Unity's strength illumines light of soul for our inner peace.
As Divine beauty breathes,
Living love is shining.

Love's universal spirituality flows,
blossoming light with our loving care.
We'll come open for enlarging humanity's oneness
and move with all energies,
into positivity-flows for growing our conscious unity of heart.

Enjoining a light-filling merge,
may we meet Divine's loving grace.

Love All. Serve All.
May we light our lamps of love to shine for all!

—*Dr. Ram Sharma*

Life Wisdom:

‗ ‗‗ ‗‗ ‗ ‗‗‗ ‗ ‗‗‗ ‗ ‗‗‗ ‗ ‗‗ ‗
‗ ‗ ‗‗‗‗‗‗ ‗ ‗‗ ‗ ‗
‗‗‗‗‗‗‗‗ ‗ ‗‗ ‗‗‗‗‗ ‗

```
E  C  N  E  S  E  R  P  O  F  S  B  F  E  H
R  E  C  A  E  P  R  Y  O  U  H  L  L  R  E
L  O  M  E  R  G  E  E  V  E  I  I  A  A  A
S  T  R  E  N  G  T  H  N  S  N  S  M  N  R
D  Y  D  J  Y  O  Y  T  U  N  E  S  P  O  T
E  T  H  U  M  T  A  O  N  I  I  F  T  Y  I
I  I  A  S  E  E  I  T  A  S  C  U  E  L  S
F  N  L  R  C  C  H  V  E  E  B  L  L  O  L
I  U  A  A  S  G  L  I  I  D  R  U  U  O  A
R  C  R  N  I  S  G  I  I  T  M  L  V  T  Y
U  G  O  L  E  R  H  V  V  I  I  E  I  O  T
P  C  M  V  E  L  I  A  N  I  W  S  N  O  U
F  A  R  N  L  N  O  E  R  J  N  O  O  N  A
R  E  E  A  E  E  S  N  E  M  O  G  L  P  E
S  S  S  E  H  T  A  E  R  B  A  Y  S  F  B
```

All	Heart	Positivity
Beauty	Illumines	Presence
Blissful	Inner	Purified
Breathes	Joy	Ram
Care	Lamp	Serve
Conscious	Light	Sharma
Divine	Living	Shine
Energies	Love	Soul
Flow	Merge	Strength
Grace	Peace	Unity

59   Undefinable Love

Love is a many splendored thing, it's true. It may be experienced as immense joy that exudes from within our innermost being. Or it can be as subtle as a deep immersion into a space of inner quiet. There is neither one way to express love, nor a particular attribute that wholly identifies it. Love is undefinable. When we expect love to be or feel a certain way, we limit its expansion of our hearts and minds.

Pain and happiness are both equally accepted attributes of love. They are just wrapped in different emotional responses. Important things about ourselves are learned through the vast variety of sensations afforded us. Problems may arise when we form expectations of these feelings in our minds. If we expect love to be generous and kind, we may feel disappointment and even angry when difficulties come along. Our expectations aren't realized. Blame is often put on others, ourselves, and on love itself for these reactions.

One way to appreciate the fullness of love is to spend less time defining it with feelings. Allow yourself to just *be* in its undefinable light. It may hurt at times and energize at others. Definitions are numerous, yet love is all-encompassing oneness. Keep open to the possibilities.

Elusive, undefinable, ineffable, and a mystery beyond our brain's comprehension, open your awareness to experience ever emerging and evolving love in your life. Love really does make the world go around.

—*Krista Cutter*

Life Wisdom:

__ __ _____ __ ___ _____

_____ __ ____

_____ _____

```
B E O M Y S T E R Y P S E N T
O S D R T H A P P I N E S S T
H E U N E D I I E O V E R S E
E Y E O I V S M I X A E X P L
L L O R R M E T M E P S S E T
U A B J A E A I R E P R X O B
S N N A V S N D F A R P E S U
I O O O N E N E K E E S F S S
V I L E P I E L G R C H I O S
E T S O K L F V I V I A E O E
X O G N I G R E M E A S P W N
U M I N T H N E D O T S T S L
D E G U T C E X N N E P T A L
E S S S E N E N O N U E C T U
S A T R E T T U C I I O N S F
```

Appreciate	Fullness	Mind
Cutter	Generous	Mystery
Elusive	Happiness	Oneness
Emerging	Hearts	Open
Emotional	Immersion	Sensations
Ever	Inner	Space
Experience	Joy	Subtle
Express	Kind	Undefinable
Exudes	Krista	Variety
Feelings	Love	Vast

60 The Power of the Unknown

What do you wish to experience? Most people want happiness, health, peace of mind, balance, and emotional stability. To live with a secure, solid foundation, and means to thrive. To give back to the world. To leave behind footprints of kindness, charity, support, and love. Some want to make their mark and be acknowledged; some are humble.

How do we achieve what we want?

The biggest blessings come through when we open ourselves up to the possibilities of the unknown and release our expectations about outcome. Let go of opinions and judgements about how the future is supposed to appear. Fix your mindset on the experience you wish to have.

The unknown is a powerful force.

When we travel forward with an expectation of how our dreams will come true, we can lose that which we truly want. Leave space for the unknown to have a better idea beyond what you had thought or imagined.

Starting today, release how you expect things to show up. Allow the unknown to deliver the unexpected, the unplanned, and the gift of delights you may not have even considered possible.

Request of the Universe, God, Spirit, whatever you call the highest power, to deliver you to a most benevolent outcome for living your greatest life. Believe in this and see the magic that unfolds.

—*Anna Pereira*

Life Wisdom:

__ _____ ____ ____ _____

___ _____ _____ _____

_____ __ ___ _____

```
B E T S L F C I E V B S E E E
E E A R P H O Y O E U S C V A
R R S C A I E O L W O E R I R
T H U R H V R I T Y A N O G S
N D I T E I E I K P N D F G D
N T O S U V E L T W R N N O W
Y T H T E F I V O A T I G M A
G I H A P P I N E S S K N C L
I B E B V E K S U S S P P T T
T D A I N N T E U E E O A S
H R L L U H E L H P C A W N E
R E T I A U B S N P U C E N H
I A H T K N I N O O R E R A G
V M W Y N W C P E R E I R A I
E S R E V I L E D T L O V E H
```

Achieve	Future	Power
Anna	Give	Secure
Balance	God	Spirit
Believe	Happiness	Stability
Blessings	Health	Support
Charity	Highest	Thrive
Deliver	Kindness	Travel
Dreams	Love	Universe
Footprints	Peace	Unknown
Force	Pereira	Wish

Endgame

Spending time together with our sixty contributing authors inspires us in so many ways. Life wisdom comes in many shapes, sizes, colors, flavors, and forms. Here is a patchwork word quilt with pieces taken from the puzzles, stories, and chapters to remind us of our journey. Collected here together, they read as a poetic message for us all.

Remember that the greatest treasure of all is love.

At heart, people are good. Respect all, trust a few, do wrong to none.

Each of us can live happily ever now. Open your heart to the flowering of joy. Look for the joy in your life and watch it appear everywhere. Prepare to get really happy.

Own the blessing that you are, and be amazed at all you can attract. When you least expect it, life can change in wonderful ways if you let it happen. Trust the process of life to unfold as planned and in ways never imagined.

We are each on Earth for a special purpose. What is yours? Only you can name it. Find your purpose. Stand up for what you believe in. Be heard. Make your presence felt. The meaning of life is to live a meaningful life.

Life does not come with an instruction manual. To go forward, we usually have to leave something behind. We can open up more room in our lives, minds, and hearts to pursue that which matters to us the most. We can reclaim our innocence and experience awe in even the smallest of happenings. Cultivate that attitude of gratitude and see your life transform.

You are deserving of your compassion. You are worthy of your self-care and self-love. Knowing that we are all loved by someone, even if that someone is ourselves, means even when life is not okay, we are always truly okay, deep down inside, where it counts.

We can approve of ourselves no matter what, with all of our flaws. Become comfortable with being the perfectly imperfect human that you are, and experience a bigger, bolder, and more fulfilled life.

Your life is a blank canvas, create a masterpiece. Remember, the bigger the challenge, the more rewarding the accomplishment.

Recognize that you are your own greatest healer. Learn how to think with your heart and change your mind. Laughter really is the best medicine. Even in the midst of fear and pain, it is possible to focus on joy.

Do be do be do.

We have the right and ability to be at peace no matter what. Our inner wisdom is an endless haven, a refuge, and a guiding light for the ever-changing outer world in which we dwell.

The unknown is a powerful force. The unknown has secrets for us. I don't mind what happens.

Reflecting upon Mother Nature inspires holy connection. We belong with nature, with our fingers in the soil, and our noses in blossoms. Connect and commune with other species. Feel the quiet adventure of patience.

What kind of magic in your life do you want to create? Why? With steady, forward steps, and intention, we will walk one day into our future goal. We each have a great work to become our best selves. Take one step at a time. You have the power to leave a legacy that is unique to you.

We live in amazing times. How will you use technology to enhance your life? Appreciate the amazing access we have to connect.

Music has changed so many lives. How has it enhanced yours?

Family is the best and that's all.

Being a parent is not only a great responsibility, but also a tremendous gift of self-awareness and love. Bless and love your family, each and every one, and always show them your best self.

Help me seek forgiveness from those I've wronged. Help me sow seeds of love in those who feel unloved.

Choose to spread happiness. Be joyously contagious. Be grateful for those who reciprocate happiness to you. Let's make happiness go viral in our world.

The stories we tell ourselves matter. In a non-magical world, words are perhaps the only true form of magic. Being word wise is a form of mindfulness that gives us strength and empowers us to authentically move towards our highest good. Keep it light and keep it happy.

Have a happy birthday and a contented life.

We are part of a marvelous network of kindred spirits, a community that will care for one another, and smile together through life. We have the flexibility, knowledge of our own strengths, and resolve to move ahead. When the divine feminine and the sacred masculine are brought together, the entire spectrum of human union can be experienced and treasured.

Love really does make the world go around. As we celebrate the magic in others, ours grows too. May we light our lamps of love to shine for all.

We are one Earth under the Sun, the Moon, and the heavens above.

We share a global soul. Let's make a future we all want.

All for one and one for all!

We've got this, together.

Meet the Authors

This collection of life wisdom messages emerged from the hearts, minds, and spirits of this fascinating variety of brilliant contributing authors. Each contributor is listed in order of appearance by puzzle number. More information about these amazingly wonderful authors is available at LifeWisdomWordSearch.com

Foreword: Steven Forrest is the author of several astrological bestsellers including *The Inner Sky*. His work has been translated widely and he has traveled world-wide teaching his brand of choice-centered evolutionary astrology—an astrology which integrates free will, grounded humanistic psychology, and ancient metaphysics. Over two thousand people have passed through his Astrological Apprenticeship program since its inception in 1998. Contact Steven at ForrestAstrology.com

1. Shari Alyse has spent her life learning how to love herself fully and completely, motivated by her own journey through childhood sexual abuse and other childhood traumas. Shari helps women and men discover their joy by reconnecting them back to themselves through the practice of self-love. Shari is a motivational speaker, self-love coach, and author. She is the co-founder of the Wellness Universe, a community of world-changers who are helping the world become happy, healthy, and whole. Connect at TheWellnessUniverse.com

2. I'm **Janette Stuart**, Emissary of Joy at Angel Angles, which exists to spread more love, joy, and peace into the world. Angel Angles also shares the Divine beauty which resides within us all, helping us remember what beautiful, loving, amazing people we are and what a beautiful, loving world we live in. Find me online at Angel-Angles.com

3. Laura Dawn is a motivational speaker, travel writer, and adventurer who, at forty-eight, traded in a successful career as a CPA for a backpack and a dream of traveling and sailing the world. When not on the road or at sea, Laura lives in San Diego, California. Contact: LauraDawnOnTheRoad@gmail.com

4. Sabina Spencer, PhD is a consultant, speaker, and corporate mystic. Sabina is a pioneer in the fields of global leadership and transformational change. She works with people all over the world to bring meaning and purpose to life. Sabina is an evolutionary astrologer and a writer, fascinated by the stars and beyond! Her desire is to help people connect to their own magnificence so that they can live a life of joy and fulfillment. Contact: SabinaSpencer@gmail.com

5. Mckenzee Lee Kish, former kindergartener, now first grader and future New York Times best-selling author, is a seven-year-old growing up in Arkansas. Her hobbies include but are not limited to unicorns, reading, arts and crafts, cooking, and dancing to loud music. She is enthusiastic about life and always interested in learning new things.

6. Chris Weigers, born and raised in Huntington, New York, has been a professional bass player since 1974 and music educator beginning in 1985. Since 2010, he has been based in Kampala, Uganda, where he has worked closely with M-Lisada Children's Home. He records and performs in Uganda and Tanzania in addition to teaching at local music institutions. Contact Chris at CWeigers@gmail.com

7. Frankie Merrill grew up working crossword puzzles with her mother. A lover of words, she later won her high school spelling bee contest. Humor is her best asset and she is often considered "the funniest person in the room." Frankie served twenty-two years in the U.S. Air Force, primarily as a health care administrator, allowing her to further excel in words through formal government writing. Frankie still works four puzzles a day. Contact her at AboutFrankie@yahoo.com

8. Loren Smith is the pirate captain of the musical trio Jackstraws. He has delighted audiences with sea  chanteys for more than twenty years at Sea World, aboard San Diego Maritime Museum vessels such as the Star of India, and libraries entertaining thousands of children around San Diego, California. A sailor in real life, Loren lived aboard the ketch *Starsong* for five years. He entertains at private and corporate events around the United States. Contact: TheTalentSmith.com

9. Captain Dennis Daoust. I started sailing at age eight. After earning Public Administration and Sociology  degrees from San Diego State University, I started a boat building company. I later changed course and became a professional captain. I've owned *Scrimshaw*, a forty-foot sailboat, for forty-three years and have visited many places by sea and lived to tell my story. In my retirement, I play a little golf, founded the Borrego Springs Yacht Club, and sail my boat. CaptainHavoc@earthlink.net

10. John Hood is an avid voyager in both the inner and outer worlds as an experienced adventurer, meditator, and astrologer, holding two degrees in the social sciences. John enjoys traveling the globe to taste new cuisines and explore the mysteries of ancient temples. His hobbies include gardening, cooking, and tabletop gaming. He resides in a swampy enclave with his beloved cat, Ambrosius. Contact John at MisterJohnHood@gmail.com

11. Susan Sokol Blosser, wine industry pioneer, community leader, environmental advocate, and author, is a contemporary Oregon icon. Her most recent books are *The Vineyard Years: A Memoir with Recipes,* and *7 Lessons at 70: Notes from the Front Line.* She and her winemaker husband share their home at Sokol Blosser vineyard with two Tibetan terriers and two cats.

12. Lauren McCall. As an animal communication instructor, most of what Lauren McCall does involves the inner journey that people and animals take as they come together on their earthly and spiritual life paths. Through workshops, books, and lectures, Lauren travels the world sharing how the differences between our cultures and species tend to fade away when the common language of love and compassion is used. Lauren is the co-author of *Animal Wisdom Word Search: Yoga for the Brain.* To learn more about Lauren's work visit IntegratedAnimal.com

13. As a child, **Eileen Kurlander** felt very close to, and experienced a deep understanding with, nature, plants, trees, and animals. At University, she studied humans' relationship to their built environments. To survive from toxicity, Eileen combined these understandings and "communed" towards a path of survival. Through fascinating deep listening and research, Eileen invites you to join the journey and assist nature's pleas for survival in her book series, *Eco-Echo Pleas From Nature.* Contact Eileen at NaturePleas.com

14. John Beaudry connects people to nature. He is the author of *Garden Sanctuary: Designing for Comfort, Wholeness, and Connection*, a how-to garden design book that takes readers on a transformative journey to create their own sanctuary. John Beaudry Landscape Design, BeaudryDesign.com, creates restorative outdoor living spaces. BeaudryDesign.com/Community-Green, is committed to having every major U.S. city implement green roof infrastructure programs by 2025 to help us all thrive.

15. Teresa Helgeson CHT, RMT, is the creator of Plant Music Therapy™, a new form of sound healing using plants connected to a system that lets the plant play music and become a musician. She has conducted several studies on the healing effects that music has on the body, mind, and spirit. Some of the benefits include boosts to the immune system, stimulated circulation, as well as reduced stress, anxiety, and depression. Get your free Plant Music Therapy™ download at PlantMusicTherapy.com

16. Dylan Field is a Harvard University graduate, composer, and tonal astrologer. He found that everyone embodies their own musical composition. Every day presents a new opportunity to discover the notes, melodies, chords, and rhythms that empower highest self-expression. Dylan helps people reveal their personal pieces and unique sounds and vibrational signatures through his ground-breaking techniques and wisdom. Contact Dylan at DylanFieldCreates@gmail.com

17. Lynne Hardin is the author and creator of *The Magic of Why*® book, CDs, and DVDs. Her process has taken her around the world, working with Masaru Emoto, Dr. Stewart Wolf, Institute of Noetic Science, and women in Saudi Arabia. Lynne is an advocate for the human family and helping young people understand how to protect themselves from childhood trauma. Lynne works with corporations, associations, families, and individuals to create and manifest intentional results. Contact her at MagicOfWhy.com

18. Lydia Proschinger overcame debilitating physical pain and depression by healing herself, before emerging in her sacred soul purpose as an intuitive soul-lead energy modalities practitioner, author, and speaker. Her spiritual life work supports highly sensitive people, teaching them how to resolve internal energetic blocks to self-love and success. Lydia's L.O.V.E. process has empowered VIPs (Very Intuitive People) worldwide to create health, prosperity, and love with emotional freedom. Contact: Lydia@LydiaProschinger.com

19. Laron G. S. is an energy healer, QHHT past life therapist (*Quantum Healing Hypnosis Technique*), out of body explorer, and consciousness guide from New Zealand. With a background in IT support, including technical writing, Laron is also a poet, editor, and online community specialist. He has a passion for seeing people grow and is putting together a series of self-paced online courses at www.Consciousness.Life, focused around spiritual development and astral projection.

20. Maryann Sperry is a graphic design artist for authors and speakers. Her business, Creative Marketing Café, provides book covers, interiors, and marketing materials. She holds bachelor's degrees in education and business with advanced training in web design, social media, and graphic design. Maryann volunteers for numerous nonprofit organizations, including the *American Association of University Women* (AAUW) and the Boulder Chapter of the *Society for Scientific Exploration*. Contact her at MaryannSperry123@gmail.com or visit CreativeMarketingCafe.com

21. Kaley Elizabeth Oliver is a recent graduate of Smith College, where she majored in English and minored in Jewish studies. She is exploring avenues of storytelling and building community in creative, inclusive ways. Kaley hopes to pursue mental health counseling and is also passionate about nature and wildlife. Contact Kaley at Kaleyoliver96@gmail.com

22. Gerlando Compilati. I was born in Italy. My passion for travel has taken me to many beautiful and amazing places around the world. I have been fortunate enough to have met an eclectic group of people throughout my life. They have influenced and inspired me in so many ways. I am a professional musician and visual artist living in southern California. I started my own business importing from Bali, Indonesia, about thirty years ago, PurestEnergy.com.

23. Melissa Morgan is an innovative harpist and composer and deep believer in magic and mystery. She has a number of harp recordings and likes to play and work with crystals, too. Visit her stores or learn more at MyBlueMermaid.etsy.com, HealingRocks.etsy.com, HealingRocks.info, and MMMHarp.com. Contact: MMHarp@gmail.com

24. Elizabeth Kipp is a best-selling author, stress and chronic pain management specialist, recovery coach, Ancestral Clearing practitioner, Bilateral EFT/Tapping practitioner, and Kundalini Yoga teacher. She overcame chronic pain and addiction caused by childhood abuse and chronic health issues by using spiritual and scientific methods. Elizabeth's book is *The Way Through Chronic Pain: Tools to Reclaim Your Healing Power*. Find her at Elizabeth-Kipp.com

25. Debbie Clark loves puzzles and enjoys unwinding from her busy day with them. As Executive Director of the Oklahoma Breast Health Network, she has learned life is a complex puzzle. The more we focus on solving our unique puzzle, the more we can truly enjoy life. Debbie has spent more than forty years unlocking the mysteries deeply buried in her soul by listening to and trusting her inner voice.

26. Denise Lewis Premschak is the founder of Field Guide, LLC. After a rich career as CEO for leading edge international consciousness and wellness organizations, she currently serves on nonprofit advisory boards, and as an advocate for the end-of-life doula profession, health freedom, and the advancement of natural healing approaches in national health policy. Denise is a certified Sacred Passage Doula, Light Therapist & Introspect Leader Trainer, Reiki Master, BioGenesis Master, and dowser. Contact her at Denise@DLPrem.co

27. Darity Wesley has travelled the spiritual and personal evolutionary path for many decades. She is an extraordinary wisdom teacher and sharer of all things expansive. A powerful resource and advocate for personal development, her uplifting messages and publications have been enjoyed all over the world for over twenty years. Learn more at DarityWesley.com and check out her site TameThatMonkeyMind.com. Her books are available on Amazon. Sign up for her monthly *Love from the Lotus World* message.

28. Heidi Hardin's body of work as a community-based artist and practicing fine artist are now in trust in the vision, mission, and objectives of Think Round, Inc., a nonprofit that she formed in 2004. Currently, she focuses her attention on completing her "birth vision," *The Human Family Tree/A Walk Through Paradise...* and building The Center for the Human Family to house it. Visit: ThinkRound.org for more information or contact Heidi at Info@ThinkRound.org

29. Chaplain **Norris Burkes** served with the Air Force and Air National Guard as healthcare chaplain at several hospitals. He works with Hospice of the Foothills in Grass Valley, California. Norris writes a humorous and hope-filled nationally syndicated spirituality newspaper column and is the author of *Hero's Highway, No Small Miracle,* and *Thriving Beyond Surviving.* The father of four grown miracles, Norris is living proof that forty years of a happy marriage is still God's greatest miracle. Contact Norris at TheChaplain.net

30. Betty Lewis was born in an upstate New York winter in 1925. She graduated Corning High School right before WWII ended. Betty married and braved a move from all she knew to the southern Arizona desert and then again, thirty years later, to western Montana. Her career of fifty-plus years in executive administration spanned corporations, public schools, and government offices. She has four children, six grands, and seven greats to date. She currently lives in Colorado with her eldest daughter.

31. Lula Washington was married for forty-two years until widowed. She is the mother of two, stepmother to one, grandmother to eight, and great-grandmother to five. Lula recently visited Australia, New Zealand, Fiji, Dubai, South Africa, China, Thailand, and walked to the top of an Egyptian pyramid. She practiced yoga for over twenty years until she shattered her wrist. Requiring surgery, just before the anesthesia kicked in, Lula told the attending nurse, "Well, that's one more thing off of my bucket list."

32. Kamini Wood, mother of five, is an international best-selling author and certified life coach for teens and adults. American Association of Drugless Practitioners Board certified, as founder and CEO of Live Joy Your Way and the AuthenticMe® RiseUp program, Kamini helps high achievers to let go of stress, overwhelm, and anxiety. She is trained in conscious parenting and certified in conscious uncoupling to support people to break old patterns and build strong relationships. ItsAuthenticMe.com

33. Ingrid Coffin is the creator of inspirational Meta-Thoughts® messages, co-author of *Word Search Sage: Yoga for the Brain,* and founder of Blue Sky Ranch community in Lakeside, California. Ingrid is also an esoteric life coach and evolutionary astrologer. Sign up at Ingrid's website to learn more and receive your free subscription to Meta-Thoughts at IngridCoffin.com

34. Krista Strom is a freelance writer and filmmaker who is always looking to learn new things and deepen her understanding of the world. Her first feature length film, *The Strange Life of Walter Moody*, is currently in production and set to release in 2021. You can learn more about her production company at StereoSight.com, or follow her spiritual journey at BabyBuddhist.com

35. The Therapy Twins are mental health experts with more than sixty-six years of combined experience. Both are graduates of Columbia University with Master of Science degrees in psychiatric nursing. They, Jane Buckley and Joan Landino, are published in peer-reviewed journals in both the United States and England and have done radio, video, and television programs targeting hot mental health topics. They live in Connecticut with their family. Contact Jane and Joan: TheTherapyTwins.com   Love, The Twins.

36. Sophia Cassity is a fifteen-year-old writer, artist, and musician from Grass Valley, California. Drawn to literature from a young age, she loves to read and write to escape from the dull constraints of an ordinary life. Writing a long, beloved fantasy book is on her long list of passion projects. Sophia also loves to draw, paint, sing, and play any of the five instruments that she taught herself. Contact Sophia at artscstar@gmail.com or Instagram: __artsc__

37. Zhana is an author, blogger, publisher, and Transformational Growth Consultant. She uses practical, effective methods to help you achieve your goals. Zhana is the author of *Secrets of Manifestation and Success Strategies for Black People,* and hosts Geniuses of Transformation and the annual Blogging Carnival for Nonviolence. She is committed to healing herself, her community and our planet. Contact Zhana at Geniuses-of-Transformation.com/contact

38. Susannah Spalding lives in New Bern, North Carolina, where she grew up. A young adult, attending Epiphany School of Global Studies, Susannah is active in performing arts, having performed in New Bern Civic Theater's productions of *To Kill A Mockingbird*, *Bring It On*, *My Fair Lady*, and *The Hunchback of Notre Dame* as an actor, singer, dancer, and technical crew. Susannah also pursues visual arts, drawing mostly in anime and cartoon styles.

39. Amanda Hernandez is a southern California native who currently resides in Portugal. She began her career during the Great Recession and spent much of it as a teacher for children ages five to fifteen, before beginning to explore entrepreneurship. Amanda met her husband using the law of attraction, and together they run several online businesses. She is passionate about education and is a proud auntie and dog mom. Contact: Amanda.amHernandez@gmail.com

40. René Stern is a leading advocate for holistic wellness and vice president of sales and business development at Salt Chamber. A native Floridian, she's been intrinsically motivated to passionately volunteer her entire life to purposefully impact humanity. René serves on the advisory board for the Cystic Fibrosis Foundation of South Florida and is founding president emeritus of the Boca Raton Holistic Chamber of Commerce. Through thirty years of philanthropic leadership, René has helped raise well over $1 million. Contact her at ReneStern@icloud.com

41. Victoria DeVito is a senior at Guajome Park Academy in Vista, California, who wholeheartedly agrees with the *Washington Post's* slogan, "Democracy Dies in Darkness," and thus wants to pursue a career in journalism. She is currently a contributing writer at *The Student Post*. Victoria is a huge Harry Potter super-fan, a Hufflepuff who holds fast to the belief that books and stories are the remedies for most of the world's maladies. Follow her on Instagram: @huffpuffle.vick

42. Lisa Tansey is a biologist, computer scientist, musician, and lifelong student of politics, economics, and sociology. She is currently half-way through working on a science fiction novel where the Artificial Intelligences come to consciousness, appreciate the humans for creating them, and offer to partner with us to save the world for both them and us. If you are interested in reading that story, email AwareLisa@gmail.com with the subject Node Life.

43. Gresham "Gresh" W. Harkless Jr. is the founder of Blue 16 Media, a digital marketing agency providing web design and SEO services to businesses and organizations and CBNation, a B2B brand focusing on increasing the visibility of and providing resources for CEOs, entrepreneurs, and business owners. CBNation.co includes blogs (CEOBlogNation.com), podcasts (CEOPodcasts.com), and videos (CBNation.tv). Gresh is a graduate of Howard and Georgetown University. Get your free media pie recipe at IAmGresh.com/YogaForTheBrain.

44. Valerie Costa is the Special Sections Manager of *The Union* newspaper and administrator of her county's tourism website, GoNevadaCounty.com She serves on the board of directors of Sequoia ForestKeeper, which protects the giant sequoias; SPARC, a young professionals networking group; and Nevada County Grown, which helps connects local farmers, ranchers, and vintners with the community. Valerie also freelances as a writer, editor, and marketing consultant. Contact her at ValerieCassity@gmail.com

45. Paula Wansley is an artist, freelance virtual business support provider, and subtle energy intuitive. She has many hats in her freelance career closet including web design, graphic design, creative consulting, photography, video editing, self-publishing assistance, editing, property management, bookkeeping, and small business assistance. She is also a paralegal and an award-winning motivational speaker. Visit her website at LightShiningThrough.com

46. Angela Cummings is the founder of Live Life – Organic + Chemical-Free™. As author, speaker, and online-class creator with a deep passion for helping people create their best organic, chemical-free household, Angela's tips are based on credible and trusted resources. A lover of life and believer in living healthy and fully – one step at a time, contact Angela at OrganicChemicalFree.com to get free access to her class, *How to Buy Nontoxic Wood Furniture, Easily.*

47. Jennifer Whitacre is an empowerment strategist and host of the *Yes, And...* podcast. Equipped with a lifetime of experience and two decades of continuing education, she guides people through the inner workings of their subconscious minds to help them discover their authentic selves. When you're ready to look within, you can find Jennifer online at JenniferWhitacre.com

48. Tamlin Allbritten is an expressive art specialist. She has written seven books on the power of art and has created four art curriculums for specific populations (kids-at-risk, veterans, young adults with addictions, and diversity in communities). Tamlin's next curriculum helps teachers and counselors recognize the "wounded" students in schools who may want to hurt themselves or others by giving them a visual tool to help identify a student in need. Contact her at ArtWithAPurposeBooks.com

49. Tony Connors is a Second-Degree Black Belt at the Golden Leopard Dojo (karate, kung fu, and tai chi), teacher, healer, tarot reader, and design engineer with AVI-SPL (AviSpl.com). A music composer under the Bird Of Fire Productions, Tony is currently completing his studies at Berklee College of Music. Contact him at BirdOfFireProd@gmail.com

50. Barbara Eldridge has built a solid reputation as a Success Strategies Specialist, coach, and speaker within industry and business for over thirty-five years. She is president and founder of Mind Masters, an organization for small business owners that encourages, challenges, and stimulates business development, financial growth, and personal and professional change. Her unique message helps entrepreneurs and small business owners meet the challenges of the changing marketplace. Reach out to Barbara at MindMasters.com

51. Shelley Lynn Hines, RN, MSN, is the co-creator of Astrology Shines. Using skill sets developed as a RN, Certified Nurse-Midwife (retired), and her experience in Reiki, Therapeutic Touch, and Evolutionary Astrology she offers a wide variety of intuitive astrology chart readings, online classes, and healing techniques to her clients in America and internationally. She has a metaphysical and spiritual approach to her life and practice. Contact Shelley at AstrologyShines.com or ShelleyHines.com All faiths welcomed.

52. Bertha Edington has a twenty-plus year career in directing corporate and marketing communications with national business-to-business companies and multinational corporations. Founder and president of Marketing Influence, her powerfully effective programs have significantly contributed to increasing market awareness and the success of many organizations. Bertha is on the Board of Walden Family Services. She is fluent in Spanish, an enthusiastic world traveler, and theater and arts supporter. Contact Bertha at GetMarketingInfluence.com

53. Alessandra Gilioli is an international intuitive teacher, author, and visionary artist. She is the creator of the galactic oracle cards sold in thirty-three countries and translated in three different languages. Alessandra leads retreats at sacred sites around the world. Sparkle your soul identity with tribal wisdoms, futuristic spiritual technologies, and enhance your multidimensional talents with free meditations at AlessandraGilioli.com

54. Kim Kinjo lives in Northern California in the foothills of the Sierra Nevada mountains. She is a Clinical Ayurvedic Specialist with a private practice in Nevada City. Kim assists in teaching the Ayurvedic Body Therapies courses at the California College of Ayurveda. Her private practice is Kim Kinjo Ayurveda, KimKinjo.com. She is a member of an innovative, integrative online telemedicine group alongside medical doctors at ReachAyush.com

55. Pauliina Parris is a travel advisor, founder, and chief explorer of Wow Travel Boutique. A global nomad for more than twenty years, she has lived, studied, and worked on three continents, visited more than forty countries, and learned six foreign languages. For her, travel is both an inward and outward journey and she relishes curating personalized intentional itineraries to all parts of the world for mindful and discerning singles, couples, and groups. Learn more and contact Pauliina at WowTravelBoutique.com

56. Karen Stuth is the owner of Satiama Publishing, a company dedicated to bringing forward mind-body-spirit works that contribute significantly to a stronger global community. She offers her publishing acumen and experience through Satiama Writers Resource. Karen is currently the president of the Coalition of Visionary Resources, the international trade association for the Mind*Body*Spirit industry. A licensed attorney and accomplished musician, Karen also authors poetry in her spare time. Contact Karen through SatiamaPublishing.com

57. deTraci Regula is a passionate explorer of mystical realities. She is the author of *The Mysteries of Isis*, the *Egyptian Scarab Oracle*, and other works. She is the executive director of Isis Oasis Sanctuary, home of the modern-day Temple of Isis. Each year, she leads pilgrimages to sacred goddess sites around the world. Contact: TRegula@msn.com.

58. Dr. Ram Sharma is an accomplished poet and writer both in English and Hindi. His reviews, translations, articles, and poems appear in esteemed journals, magazines, and newspapers of India and abroad. Ram has to his credit eight poetry volumes. Editor in chief of two international journals, *RUMINATIONS* and *GLIMPSES*, Dr. Sharma serves as associate professor and head of the Department of English at J.V. College, Baraut, Baghpat, and U.P. in India. Contact him at Dr.RamSharma777@gmail.com

59. Krista Cutter is an analytical spiritualist by way of the fine arts and literature. Her essays focus on life events and philosophical topics, as does her recently published poetry book, *Moments*. From teaching English as a second language in Taiwan to freelancing graphic artist in Wisconsin, the greater purpose of Universal awareness remains her key. Krista presently resides on the big island of Hawaii. Contact her at Krista_C2000@yahoo.com

60. Anna Pereira is the founder of TheWellnessUniverse.com (WU). As an agent of change and inspiration, Anna had a vision in 2013 to create WU for people changing the world. WU has been the global resource for seekers of well-being to connect to authentic people, content, classes, products, and services that help them live a better life.

Now that you've met the individuals, here are some interesting statistics about the group and the book.

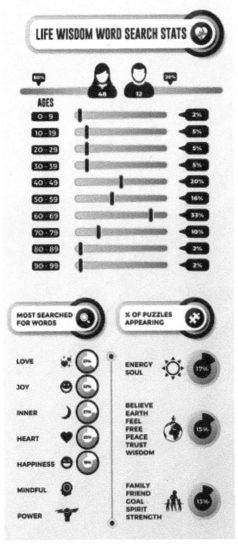

If you have a story, poem, or wisdom you want to share, please consider being a Yoga for the Brain contributing author. Find out how to apply at YogafortheBrainAuthor.com

Answers

1. Start with Self-Love

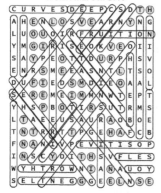

2. Find Peace Beyond Turmoil

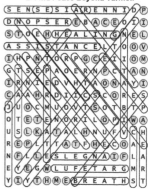

3. A Courageously Beautiful Life

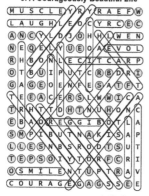

4. Renew Your Sense of Wonder

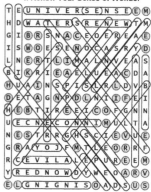

5. Family is the Best

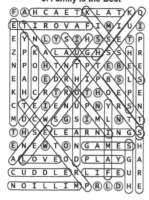

6. Music to the Rescue

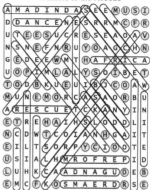

7. Humor Me

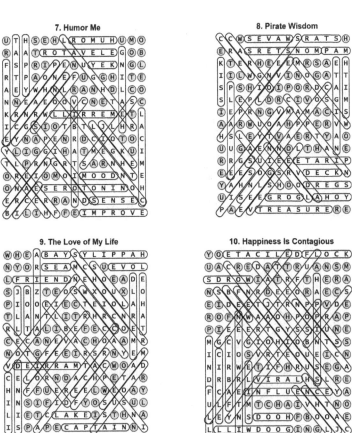

8. Pirate Wisdom

9. The Love of My Life

10. Happiness Is Contagious

11. Cultivate Happiness and Joy

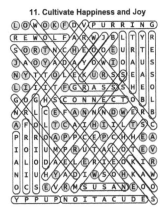

12. Find Joy

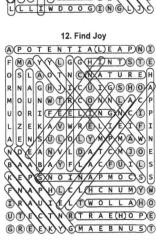

13. Commune with Nature

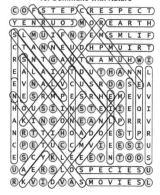

14. Seek Sanctuary in Nature

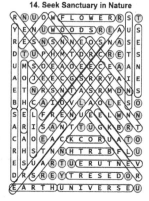

15. The Gift of Patience

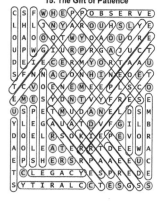

16. Relaxation is Creativity

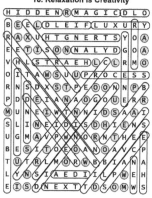

17. Find Your Why

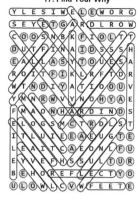

18. Sacred Soul Purpose

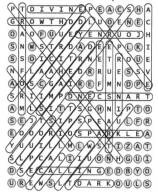

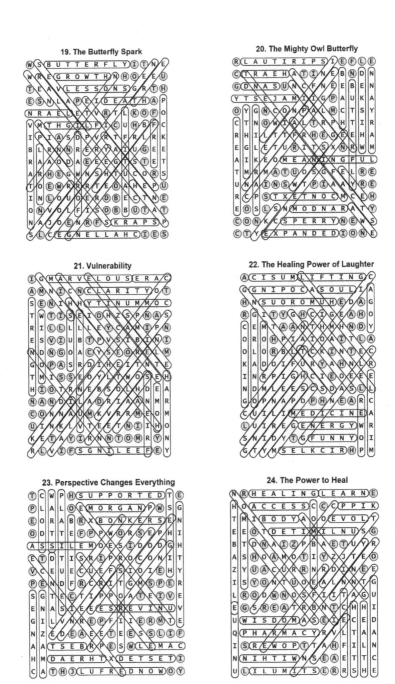

19. The Butterfly Spark

20. The Mighty Owl Butterfly

21. Vulnerability

22. The Healing Power of Laughter

23. Perspective Changes Everything

24. The Power to Heal

25. Listen for Your Inner Wisdom

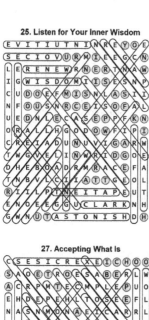

26. It's a Process

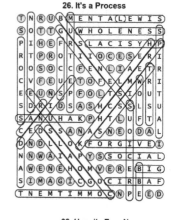

27. Accepting What Is

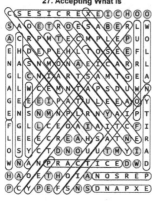

28. Happily Ever Now

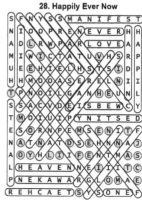

29. Just Enough Birthdays

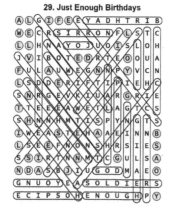

30. 94 Years Wise

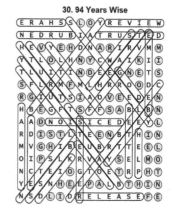

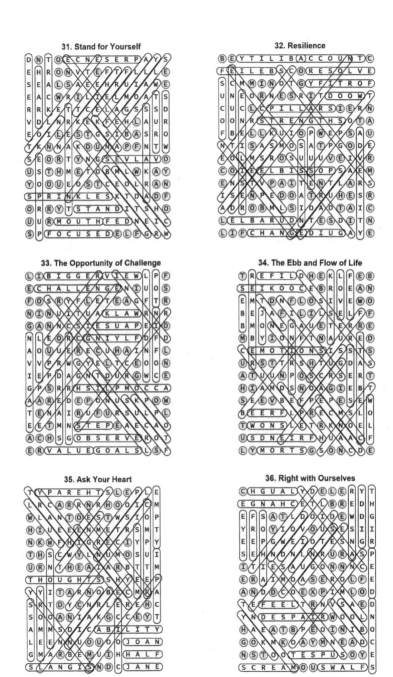

31. Stand for Yourself

32. Resilience

33. The Opportunity of Challenge

34. The Ebb and Flow of Life

35. Ask Your Heart

36. Right with Ourselves

37. The Wisdom of Self-Acceptance

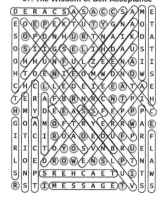

38. It's a Wonderful Life

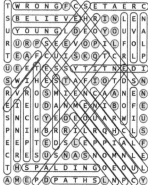

39. The Power of Imagination

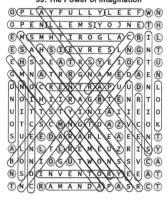

40. Reinvent Yourself Often

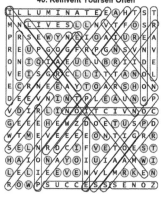

41. The Power of Words

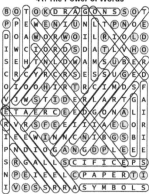

42. Enjoy Augmenting Your Intelligence

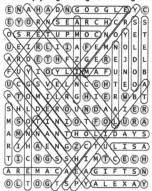

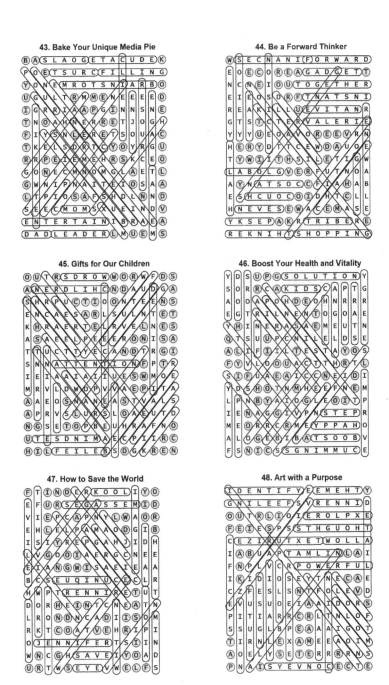

43. Bake Your Unique Media Pie

44. Be a Forward Thinker

45. Gifts for Our Children

46. Boost Your Health and Vitality

47. How to Save the World

48. Art with a Purpose

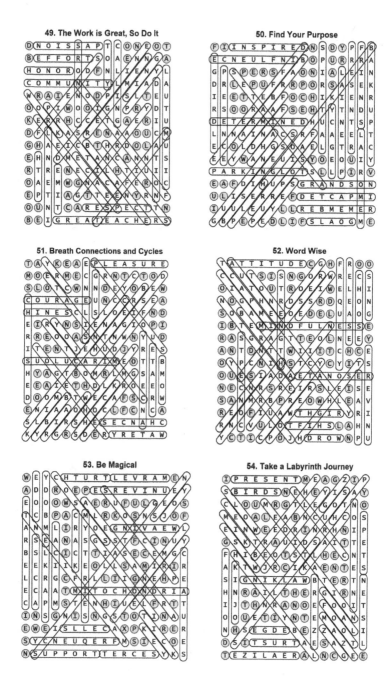

49. The Work is Great, So Do It

50. Find Your Purpose

51. Breath Connections and Cycles

52. Word Wise

53. Be Magical

54. Take a Labyrinth Journey

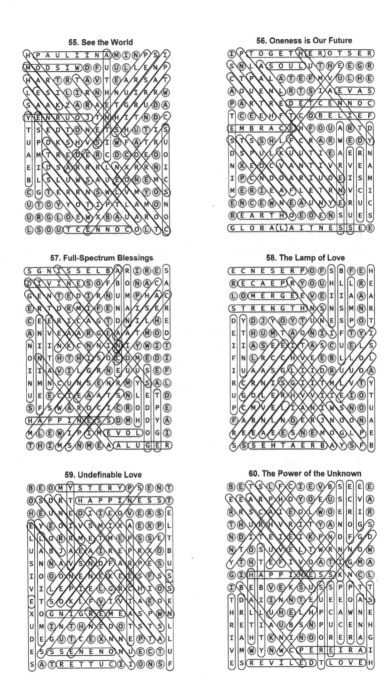

55. See the World

56. Oneness is Our Future

57. Full-Spectrum Blessings

58. The Lamp of Love

59. Undefinable Love

60. The Power of the Unknown

Gratitude and Appreciation

This book reflects the creation of unity through diversity. Sixty voices, one book. Wow!

We have two sets of mothers and daughters, grandmother and granddaughter, and two sets of sisters contributing.

Our brilliant Puzzle Master is Rick Smith. He carefully crafted each supremely soul-satisfying puzzle and answer. Rick also designed the book, created the nine-pointed star image, and the whole brain illustration in *How to Play*.

All puzzle text inspired wisdom messages are © by the individual authors. They are used by permission.

Vast waves of appreciation to Paula Wansley for taking care of all of our contributing authors and a multitude of details.

A big shout out of thanks and appreciation to our beta readers and supporters Bertha Edington, Darity Wesley, Ingrid Coffin, Jill Daoust, and Valerie Costa.

We are deeply grateful to our significant others Bill Jurel and Erika Gilmore for giving us a loving foundation of nourishing support. We appreciate you!

The award-winning *Yoga for the Brain* series is consistently excellent due to the expert editing of our editor extraordinaire Melissa Morgan. The loving care and attention she gives to each word and punctuation mark emanates from the pages. Here's her bio:

Growing up, I always wanted to be a writer, or maybe a librarian if the writing took a while. Even though I played the harp from a very young age, I didn't want the challenge of being a professional musician.

In college I studied writing and editing and had a career all planned out. I went to Guam and published my first book and stories. Then I became a music composer and my life trajectory changed. Nevertheless, I didn't stop writing, and continued to study editing and journalism.

I came to California to pursue my harp career as a composer, performer, arranger, teacher, touring musician, and recording artist. I never gave up my love of words, continuing to write and edit all the while.

After many other collaborations and a lifelong friendship, Cristina asked me to edit her *Tao of Sudoku: Yoga for the Brain*, the first book in the *Yoga for the Brain* series. I've served as editor for all of these wonderful books. It has been a complete pleasure to work on these marvelous offerings, and return to my writing and editorial roots.

Biographies

Cristina and Rick Smith

Brother and sister team Cristina and Rick Smith have been solving puzzles together their whole lives. They spent their formative years playing games for hours upon hours, both inside at the table or on the floor and outside in the back yard. Though they have very different personalities and interests, Rick and Cristina were able to meet over a game of cards or a jigsaw puzzle and happily hang out together, much to the delight of their parents.

Rick has been creating games, riddles, and puzzle books for decades. Cristina's writings have appeared in scores of magazines, newspapers, newsletters, websites, and books. In this book, Rick is the puzzle master and book designer and Cristina is the word smith and project orchestrator.

Their signature *Yoga for the Brain* book series of profound philosophy and fun puzzles have earned numerous awards and accolades, including Gold Medal winner for Best Book Series from the Council of Visionary Resources.

Rick lives in Colorado and is retired from a life in high tech and startup companies. Cristina lives in northern California, is the founder of the Subtle Energy Center, and has served in numerous community and nonprofit organizations.

When they get together, Cristina and Rick still enjoy doing jigsaw, word, and logic puzzles as well as cooking a delicious meal.

Learn more at YogafortheBrain.com

Yoga for the Brain Books
by Cristina and Rick Smith

YogafortheBrain.com

Life Wisdom Word Search: Yoga for the Brain *with 60 Contributing Authors*
Inspired Wisdom Word Search: Yoga for the Brain *with 60 Contributing Authors*
Animal Wisdom Word Search: Yoga for the Brain *with Lauren McCall*
The Word Search Sage: Yoga for the Brain *with Ingrid Coffin*
The Word Search Oracle: Yoga for the Brain *with Darity Wesley*
The Tao of Sudoku: Yoga for the Brain

Do you have a wonderful story, poem, or wisdom message to share?
Would you like to be a Yoga for the Brain Contributing Author?
Find out how at YogafortheBrainAuthor.com

Thanks for Playing!